BIBLICAL PERFORMANCES FOR EARLY CHILDHOOD

Compiled by Rebecca Daniel

Illustrated by Corbin Hillam

Cover by Janet Skiles

Shining Star Publications, Copyright © 1990
A Division of Good Apple, Inc.

ISBN No. 0-86653-548-9

Standardized Subject Code TA ac

Printing No. 9876

**Shining Star Publications
A Division of Good Apple, Inc.
1204 Buchanan St., Box 299
Carthage, IL 62321-0299**

The purchase of this book entitles the buyer to reproduce student activity pages for classroom use only. Any other use requires the written permission of Shining Star Publications.

All rights reserved. Printed in the United States of America.

Unless otherwise indicated, the King James Version of the Bible was used in preparing the activities in this book.

TO THE TEACHER/PARENT

Most youngsters love to perform. From the time babies become aware of themselves as individuals, they delight in entertaining those around them. Being loved by family, adored by parents, and applauded by all is a basic human need. Teaching Christian values through dramatic play is a natural and fun-filled experience for all involved.

When working with preschoolers, ages three or four, choose a short selection for initial performances. Using a narrator for the speaking parts while children pantomime the actions is a good way to begin. Speaking performances should be well rehearsed and brief enough that each child can remember his/her lines. Using familiar tunes to sing new songs is also a good way to get the very young learner involved on stage. When working with kindergarten children, ages five or six, slightly longer performances may be planned. These children can usually handle the two-page plays or stringing together a series of short skits, songs or finger plays.

Keep costumes and props simple. If costumes become too elaborate and the scenery and props too complicated it will detract from the overall beauty of the performance. To keep costs down, use costumes made from things you have on hand or ask for donations before you buy anything. Use your imagination. The best source of ideas is right in your head. Colored trash bags make quick biblical robes. Cut a hole in the top for the head to fit through and a hole on each side for the armholes. Gather at the waist with a rope, string or pretty scarf tied loosely. Animals may be played by having children wear paper plate or paper bag masks that they have created. If you need more elaborate costuming, ask some parents to come up with what you need. Keep and store all costumes carefully so they may be used again and again. A box of costumes in the corner of the classroom is the perfect invitation for a youngster to playact.

Give your Bible children many opportunities to stand in the spotlight with the big selection of biblical finger plays, action songs, familiar tunes, skits, pantomimes and plays found herein. Performing Bible stories will build Christian character and also help set a stage on which students can develop positive self-images.

TABLE OF CONTENTS

Finger Plays and Action Songs	3
Familiar Tunes and Songs	25
Choral Readings and Pantomimes	47
Skits and Plays	61

FINGER PLAYS AND ACTION SONGS

RHYTHMIC AND DRAMATIC ACTION
by Helen Kitchell Evans 4
DID YOU EVER SEE?
by Marcia Hornok 5
RECEIVE HIM
by Laura Cordova 7
SERVANTS OF THE LORD
by Marcia Hornok 8
SONG ABOUT DANIEL
by Marcia Hornok 8
DO YOU KNOW A BIBLE VERSE?
by Marcia Hornok 9
HOW WE WORSHIP
by Marcia Hornok 9
HOW HE LOVES ME
by Marcia Hornok 10
GOD DELIVERS THEM
by Marcia Hornok 10
GIDEON
by Patsy J. Taylor 11
SAY YOUR PRAYERS
by Kathy Darling 11
DANIEL, DANIEL, WHERE ARE YOU?
by Marilyn Senterfitt 12
COME AND FOLLOW ME
by Helen Kitchell Evans 12
FRIENDS WE'LL ALWAYS BE
by Helen Kitchell Evans 12
GOD'S PLAN
by Edith E. Cutting 13
LEAVES
by Edith E. Cutting 13
GOD MADE ONE AND ALL
by Kathy Darling 14
GOODNIGHT, LORD
by Kathy Darling 14

THE ARK THAT NOAH BUILT
by Louise Hannah Kohr 15
BIBLE CHANT
by Marcia Hornok 17
JESUS' SONG
by Marcia Hornok 17
LOST SHEEP
by Laura Cordova 18
LOVE BUG
by Susan Schneck and Mary Strohl 19
THE WONDER OF IT
by Louise Hannah Kohr 19
IMAGINATION
by Kathy Darling 20
SHOUT HOORAY!
by Kathy Darling 20
THE GREAT CATCH OF FISH
by Edith E. Cutting 21
CALMING THE SEA
by Edith E. Cutting 21
THE MAN FROM THE ROOF
by Edith E. Cutting 22
FEEDING FIVE THOUSAND
by Edith E. Cutting 22
GOD'S CARE
by Karin Glenn 23
GOD MADE ME
by Edith E. Cutting 24
THANKSGIVING GIVING
by Edith E. Cutting 24

RHYTHMIC AND DRAMATIC ACTION

by Helen Kitchell Evans

Songs that call for a rhythmic response are delightful for small children. Dramatic action helps bring out the meaning. In rhythmic responses lie many values, of which one is expressional; that is, the child has an opportunity, as in dramatization, to give outward expression to the feelings and ideas produced by the song.

Children naturally love rhythm. They make up chants and skip to rope rhymes. Another value lies in the opportunity to build improved muscular coordination. Very young children, as we all know, may be very clumsy. Experience with responding rhythmically with the hands, feet or entire body can do much to develop grace and dexterity.

The classroom often places too much emphasis on sitting. With this, a child becomes restless and circulation is slowed down. Sharing rhythms give the opportunity to move about in a purposeful and orderly fashion. Using the variety of rhythms in this book will give children hours of fun and learning.

Children usually respond voluntarily and happily to the opportunity to "playact" to music. Others will join in. The timid and reserved may subtly be led to express themselves if more responsive friends offer them a hand when starting out to skip, hop, march or otherwise do the suggested actions. Often the teacher can be a partner to the retiring child, but she must never force the child or embarrass him/her by too much insistence.

Gifted children may improvise and suggest other actions. Encourage them to do so for this gives them great confidence to see their friends doing their ideas or rhythmic interpretations.

So let rhythms be considered an important part of the daily program. Their values far outweigh the time that might be considered lost in this type of activity.

DID YOU EVER SEE?

by Marcia Hornok

Sung to: "Did You Ever See a Lassie?"

WORDS

Did you ever see strong Samson?
Strong Samson?
Strong Samson?
Did you ever see strong Samson
Fight this way and that?

Fight this way and that way;
Fight this way and that way?

Did you ever see strong Samson
Fight this way and that?

Did you ever see King David?
King David?
King David?
Did you ever see King David
Dance unto the Lord?

Dance this way and that way;
Dance this way and that way?

Did you ever see King David
Dance unto the Lord?

MOTIONS

Flex your muscle and feel it with your other hand.

Some children make fencing motions. Some children make boxing motions. Continue through end of verse.

Freestyle dancing or a clap and hop, turn around type of step that everyone does together (nearly!). Continue to end of verse.

Shining Star Publications, Copyright © 1990, A division of Good Apple, Inc.

SS1872

Did you ever see sick Naaman?
Sick Naaman?
Sick Naaman?
Did you ever see sick Naaman
Dip over his head?

Dip this way and that way;
Dip this way and that way?

Did you ever see sick Naaman
Dip over his head?

Touch hand to forehead as if feverish.

Hold nose and squat; come back up. Continue through end of verse.

Did you ever see old Jonah?
Old Jonah?
Old Jonah?
Did you ever see old Jonah
Ride in a big fish?

Ride this way and that way
Ride this way and that way?

Did you ever see old Jonah
Ride in a big fish?

Cross arms over chest and sway back and forth. Continue through end of verse.

Did you ever see Zacchaeus?
Zacchaeus?
Zacchaeus?
Did you ever see Zacchaeus
Climb a sycamore tree?

Climb this way and that way;
Climb this way and that way?

Did you ever see Zacchaeus
Climb a sycamore tree?

Hold out one hand, palm down to indicate a short person.

Move arms and feet in climbing motion. Continue through end of verse.

Did you ever see kind Dorcas?
Kind Dorcas?
Kind Dorcas?
Did you ever see kind Dorcas
Sew clothes for the poor?

Sew this way and that way;
Sew this way and that way?

Did you ever see kind Dorcas
Sew clothes for the poor?

Hold a pretend needle with one hand and move it up and down as if hemming cloth. Continue to end of verse.

RECEIVE HIM

by Laura Cordova

" . . . as many as received Him, to them gave He power to become sons of God, . . ."	(Move index fingers to left.) **AS**	(Open and close hands quickly.) **MANY**	(Move index fingers to left.) **AS**
(Open hands then close.) **RECEIVED**	(Touch head, point up.) **HIM**	(Touch fingers.) **TO**	(Point to "them.") **THEM**
(Open both hands.) **GAVE**	(Touch head, point up.) **HE**	(Move fists down.) **POWER**	(Rotate hands.) **TO BECOME**
(Touch head, place hand in arm.) **SONS**	(Link thumbs and index fingers.) **OF**	(Point up, bring open hand down.) **GOD**	John 1:29

SERVANTS OF THE LORD

by Marcia Hornok

Sung to: "I'm a Little Teapot"

WORDS	MOTIONS

David was a servant of the Lord.
   Here is his sling, and
   Here is his sword.
When he killed Goliath,
   Hear him shout,
"I trust in God without a doubt."
	One arm makes circling motion over head.
	Draw a pretend sword and hold it up.
	Cup hands at mouth.
	On "trust," clap once; then point to heaven with one hand.

David was a servant of the Lord.
   Here is his crown, and
   Here is his sword.
When he ruled the kingdom,
   Hear him shout,
"I trust in God without a doubt."
	Hands on top of head, forming a crown with fingers up.
	Draw your sword.
	Cup hands at mouth.
	Clap and point.

I can be a servant of the Lord.
   Here is my heart, and
   Here is my sword.
When I do what's right then
   Hear me shout,
"I trust in God without a doubt."
	Point to self.
	Hands crossed over heart.
	Open hands, palms up, as if holding Bible.
	Cup hands at mouth.
	Clap and point.

SONG ABOUT DANIEL

by Marcia Hornok

Sung to: "Mary Had a Little Lamb"

WORDS	MOTIONS
Daniel was a man of prayer, Man of prayer, man of prayer. Daniel was a man of prayer. God was pleased with Daniel.	Hands in "praying hands" position.
Laws were made you could not pray, Could not pray, could not pray. Laws were made you could not pray. "Nevermind," said Daniel.	Shake head no, and wave hands over each other, palms down.
Daniel in the lion's den, Lion's den, lion's den. Daniel in the lion's den. God protected Daniel.	Arms folded across chest, showing confidence (in God).
Daniel was a man of prayer, Man of prayer, man of prayer. Daniel was a man of prayer. We could be like Daniel.	Hands in "praying hands" position. Point to self.

DO YOU KNOW A BIBLE VERSE?

by Marcia Hornok
Sung to: "The Muffin Man"

Children hold hands and circle around <u>teacher</u> as she sings:

1. Oh, do you know a Bible verse, a Bible verse, a Bible verse?
   Oh, do you know a Bible verse, that's in your heart to stay?

<u>Children</u> sing:

2. Oh, yes I know a Bible verse, a Bible verse, a Bible verse.
   Oh, yes I know a Bible verse, that's in my heart to stay.

Child comes into center and recites verse from memory. More than one child may recite together. Then <u>children in middle</u> sing:

3. Now four of us know a Bible verse, a Bible verse, a Bible verse.
   Now four of us know a Bible verse, that's in our hearts to stay.

   (Repeat vs. 1: Oh, do you know a Bible verse?)

<u>Children circling</u> sing second verse.

More children come into center and recite their verse. Then all in center sing verse three. (Now more of us know a Bible verse . . . .)

After <u>all children</u> have quoted the verse, sing final verse of song:

4. Now we all know a Bible verse, a Bible verse, a Bible verse.
   Now we all know a Bible verse, that's in our hearts to stay.

HOW WE WORSHIP

by Marcia Hornok
Sung to: "Here We Go 'Round the Mulberry Bush"

WORDS	MOTIONS
This is the way we go to church, Go to church, go to church. This is the way we go to church, Every Sunday morning.	Walk in place, swinging arms.
This is the way we read God's Word, etc.	Hold hands together, palms up and look at palms.
This is the way we say our prayers, etc.	Palms together, head bowed.
This is the way we praise His name, etc.	Clap hands.
This is the way we show our love, etc.	Shake hands with each other or hug each other.

(Children may be coached to think of other things to sing about).

HOW HE LOVES ME

by Marcia Hornok

Sung to: "London Bridge"

Jesus lives in my heart,* in my heart,* in my heart.

Jesus lives in my heart.*

How He loves me.   *Point to heart

(Name other places and make appropriate action. Example: head, my house, my room, etc.)

GOD DELIVERS THEM

by Marcia Hornok

Sung to: "When Johnny Comes Marching Home Again"

Clap hands where indicated by *

See Israel down in Egypt land.
Oh my. * * Oh my. * *
See Israel down in Egypt land.
Oh my. * * Oh my. * *
See Israel down in Egypt land;
They can't escape from Pharaoh's hand.
But they all sing praise when God de-li-vers them.
 *   *   *   *   *   *   *

See Israel at the Red Sea wall.
Oh my. * * Oh my. * *
See Israel at the Red Sea wall.
Oh my. * * Oh my. * *
See Israel at the Red Sea wall.
It opens for them like a hall.
And they all sing praise when God de-li-vers them.
 *   *   *   *   *   *   *

When Israel gets into a mess.
Oh my. * * Oh my. * *
When Israel gets into a mess.
Oh my. * * Oh my. * *
When Israel gets into a mess,
If they obey, then God will bless;
And they all sing praise when God de-li-vers them.
 *   *   *   *   *   *   *

GIDEON

by Patsy J. Taylor

Sung to: "Daddy's Going to Buy Me a Mockingbird"

1. Gideon, Gideon, answer me.
   Gideon, Gideon, answer me.
   Gideon, Gideon, answer me,
   For, I have a job for you.

2. Who am I, that you'd use me?
   Who am I, that you'd use me?
   Who am I, that you'd use me?
   I'm just Gideon.

3. I will put a fleece on the floor.
   I will put a fleece on the floor.
   I will put a fleece on the floor.
   If it is wet, I'll know.

4. It is wet and I still don't know.
   It is wet and I still don't know.
   It is wet and I still don't know.
   So I will try again.

5. Th-is time it must be dry.
   Th-is time it must be dry.
   Th-is time it must be dry.
   And then I'll know for sure.

6. God's with me and we will win.
   God's with me and we will win.
   God's with me and we will win,
   Because my Lord said so.
   (Shout) WE WIN!

SAY YOUR PRAYERS

by Kathy Darling

Sung to: "If You're Happy and You Know It"

If you want to say your prayers, fold your hands. (Fold hands.)

If you're happy with your day, thank the Lord. (Blow a kiss.)

If you're thankful to the Lord,

Then you really ought to show it.

If you're thankful to the Lord, say Amen. (Whisper "Amen.")

If you're sleepy and you know it, give a yawn. (Yawn.)

If you're sleepy and you know it, say good night. (Whisper "Good night.")

If you're sleepy and you know it,

Then you really ought to show it.

If you're sleepy and you know it, close your eyes. (Close eyes.)

DANIEL, DANIEL, WHERE ARE YOU?

by Marilyn Senterfitt

Sung to: "Twinkle, Twinkle, Little Star"

WORDS	MOTIONS
Daniel, Daniel, where are you?	Place hand over eyes.
How I really wish I knew.	Place hand over eyes.
I have looked both high and low.	Point to sky and ground.
I have looked both to and fro.	Point to left and right.
Daniel, Daniel where are you?	Place hand over eyes.
Are you at a barbecue?	Motion as if eating.
I am in the lions' den.	Hold up one hand.
I was put here by some men.	Motion as if being thrown.
They said it was wrong to pray.	Bow head.
I'm a lion's meal today!	Motion as if eating.
Here I am as you can see.	Hold up one hand.
Will God above rescue me?	Look up at sky.
Daniel, Daniel, yes, He will.	Nod head "yes".
God has a plan to fulfill.	Point to sky.
An angel will come to you;	Motion as if flying.
Close the lions' mouths with glue.	Place finger across lips.
Daniel, Daniel you are free!	Hold arms straight out.
The lions will go hungry!	Hold arms straight out.

COME AND FOLLOW ME

by Helen Kitchell Evans

Sung to: "Farmer in the Dell"

Oh, come and follow me,
Oh, come and follow me,
Just do as I do now
Just follow what you see.
(Child makes a motion that others must imitate.)

FRIENDS WE'LL ALWAYS BE

by Helen Kitchell Evans

Sung to: "Farmer in the Dell"

Hello, hello from me (point to self).
My name is (child's name) you see;
So let's shake hands together now (extend hand to partner)
And friends we'll always be.

GOD'S PLAN

by Edith E. Cutting

WORDS	MOTIONS
After the rain	Fingers come wiggling down.
Comes the rainbow.	One arm makes a wide arch.
After the clouds	Hands cover the face.
Comes the sun.	Face comes out smiling.
After the bud	Hands together to make oval closed bud.
Comes the flower.	Hands open like petals.
God's plan	Join hands above head as if cheering.
Is a wonderful one!	
After the egg	Hands together in rounded form.
Comes the chicken.	Open hands as if holding baby chick.
After the night	Eyes closed, face leans on hands.
Comes the day.	Eyes open and head rises.
After the hurt	One hand over hurt place on other.
Comes the kisses.	Kiss the hurt hand.
God works	Join hands above head as if cheering.
In a wonderful way!	

LEAVES

by Edith E. Cutting

One narrator at side, with any number of children participating.

God made green leaves to give us shade,
   (Arms above head with fingers interlaced.)
And when their work was done,
   (Separate hands and lower arms.)
He painted them all yellow and red
   (Hold up one hand and make painting motions with other.)
And told them to have fun.
   (Fingers at each corner of mouth to make smiling faces.)

They swayed and sailed on the little breeze,
   (Move arms and bodies in gentle swaying.)
And the big wind made them run.
   (Stamp feet as if running, or if space permits, they may run.)
They danced and pranced and whirled and twirled
   (Dance and circle around.)
And they glittered in the sun.
   (Lift arms.)

At last they were tired, and they all fell down,
   (All lie down. Narrator walks forward.)
But I could hear everyone,
   (Narrator's hand at ear.)
As they whispered and rustled and crackled and crunched.
   (Children whisper, tap fingers and heels on floor, etc.)
God smiled that they still had fun!
   (All sit up and make smiling faces again.)

GOD MADE ONE AND ALL

by Kathy Darling

God made His children,

Man, woman, boy and girl.

Stomp . . . clap . . . give a twirl! (Stomp twice, clap twice, turn around.)

God made His creatures,

Lions, and tigers, and bears that growl!

Stomp . . . clap . . . give a howl! (Stomp twice, clap twice, howl.)

God made His creatures,

Goose, chicken, rooster, and duck.

Stomp . . . clap . . . give a cluck! (Stomp twice, clap twice, cluck.)

God made His creatures,

Birds that fly, chicks that cheep!

Stomp . . . clap . . . give a peep! (Stomp twice, clap twice, peep.)

God made His creatures,

Some are big, some are small.

Thank you, God, for one and all!

Stomp . . . clap . . . give a cheer! (Stomp twice, clap twice, cheer.)

GOODNIGHT, LORD

by Kathy Darling

WORDS	MOTIONS
Goodnight, Lord,	
It's the end of day.	Climb into bed.
I fluff my pillow,	Fluff pillow.
And pull the shade.	Pretend to pull shade.
Goodnight, Lord.	
I stretch and yawn.	Stretch and yawn.
I'll close my eyes,	Lay head down.
And see you in the dawn.	Close eyes.

THE ARK THAT NOAH BUILT

by Louise Hannah Kohr

Recited to the meter of: "This Is the House that Jack Built"

This is the Ark
That Noah built.
(everyone's finger-tips together
  to form the roof of the ark)

This is the wheat
(hand cupped to hold wheat)
Stored in the Ark
That Noah built.

This is the mouse
   (squeak, squeak)
That nibbled the wheat
Stored in the Ark
That Noah built.

This is the cat
   (meow, meow)
That chased the mouse
That nibbled the wheat
Stored in the Ark
That Noah built.

This is the dog
   (bow-wow, or waggle-waggle)
That teased the cat
That chased the mouse
That nibbled the wheat
Stored in the ark
That Noah built.

This is the goat
With a beard like Noah's,
That waggled its beard
   (waggle, waggle)
At the dog,
That teased the cat
That chased the mouse
That nibbled the wheat
Stored in the Ark
That Noah built.

This is the duck
   (quack, quack)
That followed the goat
With a beard like Noah's,
To pick up the wheat
Dropped by the goat,
That waggled its beard
   (waggle, waggle)
At the dog,
That teased the cat
That chased the mouse
That nibbled the wheat
Stored in the Ark
That Noah built.

This is the pig
   (squeal, squeal)
That followed the duck,
That followed the goat
With a beard like Noah's,
To pick up the wheat
Dropped by the goat,
That waggled its beard
At the dog,
That teased the cat
That chased the mouse
That nibbled the wheat
Stored in the Ark
That Noah built.

This is the lamb
All white and fluffy,
  (baa, baa)
That followed the pig
That followed the duck
That followed the goat
With a beard like Noah's,
To pick up the wheat
Dropped by the goat,
That waggled its beard
At the dog,
That teased the cat
That chased the mouse
That nibbled the wheat
Stored in the Ark
That Noah built.

This is the cow
That gave some milk,
To feed the lamb,
All white and fluffy,
That followed the pig
That followed the duck
That followed the goat
With a beard like Noah's,
To pick up the wheat
Dropped by the goat,
That waggled its beard
At the dog,
That teased the cat
That chased the mouse
That nibbled the wheat
Stored in the Ark
That Noah built.

This is the wife
That Noah wed,
  (curtsy, curtsy)
Who milked the cow
That gave some milk,
To feed the lamb,
All white and fluffy,
That followed the pig
That followed the duck
That followed the goat
With a beard like Noah's,
That followed the dog
That teased the cat
That chased the mouse
That nibbled the wheat
Stored in the Ark
That Noah built.

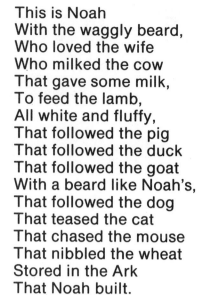

This is Noah
With the waggly beard,
Who loved the wife
Who milked the cow
That gave some milk,
To feed the lamb,
All white and fluffy,
That followed the pig
That followed the duck
That followed the goat
With a beard like Noah's,
That followed the dog
That teased the cat
That chased the mouse
That nibbled the wheat
Stored in the Ark
That Noah built.

This is the rain
  (rain, rain)
That came splashing down,
That God sent
As He said He would.
This is Noah
With the waggly beard
Who built the Ark
To save the wife
Who milked the cow,
That gave the milk
To feed the lamb,
All white and fluffy,
That followed the pig
That followed the goat
With a beard like Noah's,
That followed the dog
That teased the cat
That chased the mouse
That nibbled the wheat
Stored in the Ark
That Noah built.

This is the rainbow,
In the sky,
That followed the Ark
When the earth was dry,
A promise to all
That there never would be,
Such a flood
As that when the
Animals went two-by-two
Into the Ark
That Noah built.

BIBLE CHANT

by Marcia Hornok

March to the beat while speaking. If children are coordinated enough, they can also swing their arms.

The Bible. The Bible.
God wants me to know.

The Bible. The Bible.
That's how I can grow.

The Bible. The Bible.
Spell it with a "B."

The Bible. The Bible.
Is the book for ME.

B—I—B—L—E (Stop marching, clap with each letter.)

JESUS' SONG

by Marcia Hornok

This finger play can be sung to: "Old MacDonald Had a Farm"

Jesus came to earth for me.
*I love Him the best.

Died and rose again for me.
*I love Him the best.

*With love, love here, and love, love there.
*Here love, there love, everywhere love, love.

Jesus is my favorite friend.
*I love Him the best.

*Younger children may sing only the starred lines.

Motions: Every time child sings the word, "Love," he can either point to his/her chest or make a heart shape one of three ways:

1. With 2 hands held together, fingers curved at top, thumbs touching at bottom.

2. Arms form a heart with fingers resting at top of head.

3. With index fingers tracing heart pattern in the air.
   (Song moves too fast to do this without confusion, thus adding to the fun!)

LOST SHEEP

by Laura Cordova

Teacher asks the questions. Children clap and count the answer. * indicates claps. Use this at the end of a program.

When learning this exercise, do it in the order given. After it is well-learned, you may give them in any order, to increase children's listening skills.

Teacher	Children
How many sheep were lost?	* 1
How many people lived in the Garden of Eden?	* * 1-2
How many times a day did Daniel pray?	* * * 1-2-3
How many friends carried a crippled man to Jesus?	* * * * 1-2-3-4
How many smooth stones did David pick up?	* * * * * 1-2-3-4-5
In how many days did God create the world?	* * * * * * 1-2-3-4-5-6
How many churches did John write to?	* * * * * * * 1-2-3-4-5-6-7
How many people were on the ark?	* * * * * * * * 1-2-3-4-5-6-7-8
How many men forgot to thank Jesus after He healed them?	* * * * * * * * * 1-2-3-4-5-6-7-8-9
How many young girls carried a lamp to a wedding?	* * * * * * * * * * 1-2-3-4-5-6-7-8-9-10
How many disciples saw Jesus after His resurrection?	* * * * * * * * * * * 1-2-3-4-5-6-7-8-9-10-11
How many sons did Israel have?	* * * * * * * * * * * * 1-2-3-4-5-6-7-8-9-10-11-12
How many people does Jesus love?	Children clap wildly, as fast and as loud as possible.

LOVE BUG

by Susan Schneck and
Mary Strohl

It begins with a grin,
  (*Smile broadly.*)
It turns in to a giggle.
  (*Put both hands on mouth, giggle.*)
You start to laugh.
  (*Throw head back, laugh out loud.*)
Your legs start to wiggle!
  (*Put feet in air and shake.
  Alternative: If your shoes are off, you can say, "Your toes start to wiggle."*)
You look all around for someone to hug.
  (*Move eyes back and forth.*)
What can you do?
  (*Shrug shoulders.*)
You've caught the LOVE BUG!
  (*Hug your partner, teacher, mom or dad!*)
ACHOOO!

THE WONDER OF IT

by Louise Hannah Kohr

God made the big round sun.
  (Put arms in circle over head.)

He made the clouds on high.
  (Spread arms high and wide.)

Little things that hop and run—
  (Make hopping motions with fingers, run fingers up arms.)

He made the birds that fly.
  (Make flying motions.)

God made the mountains;
  (Place hands together, tent fashion, for mountains.)

He made the deep blue sea.

And then, because He loved so much, He made you and He made me.
  (Point to you and me.)

IMAGINATION

by Kathy Darling

God gave me an imagination, (Tap head.)

So I can be anything in His creation. (Circle arms wide.)

I can growl and claw like an angry bear. (Make claws and growl.)

I can swim like a fish, or hop like a hare. (Stroke arms, then hop.)

I can slither and slide like a long black snake. (Slither on the floor.)

I can waddle and quack like a duck on a lake. (Waddle around and quack.)

I can drive a car or captain a boat. (Steer the wheel.)

Or charge like a knight across the castle moat. (Gallop on horse.)

I can be a doctor, or study the stars. (Look through telescope to stars.)

I can sail the seas, or travel space to Mars. (Salute, then point to sky.)

I can be anything in God's creation. (Circle arms wide.)

Thank you, God, for imagination! (Tap head.)

SHOUT HOORAY!

by Kathy Darling

To my Lord, I give all of me. (Spread arms wide.)

Clap my hands, slap my knee. (Clap twice and slap.)

To my Lord, I give my face. (Point to face.)

Put a smile on that special place. (Make a grin.)

To my Lord, I give my love. (Put hands over heart.)

Raise my arms up high above. (Raise arms high.)

To my Lord, I give my voice. (Place hands on throat.)

Shout hoo-ray, let's rejoice! (Shout hoo-ray!)

THE GREAT CATCH OF FISH

by Edith E. Cutting

Peter was a fisherman
   (Stand tall.)
With his boat on Galilee.
   (Put hands together scooped like a boat.)
One night he didn't catch any fish.
   (Shake head and turn hands upside down.)
He was sad as he could be.
   (Put fingers at corners of mouth and pull down.)

His good friend, Jesus, said to him,
   (Put hand over heart.)
"Go back where the water is deep.
   (Extend arm and finger to point.)
Throw out your nets and you will catch
   (Spread both hands in tossing motion.)
All the fish you want to keep."
   (Bring arms up as if holding a big bundle.)

Peter threw the fishnets out
   (Spread out hands in tossing motion.)
And just as quick as a wink
   (Wink both eyes.)
He caught so many, many fish
   (Reach out, pull back as if pulling nets in.)
His boat began to sink.
   (Squat down as if going down in water.)

Peter was so surprised and scared
   (Look over one shoulder, then the other.)
He knelt by Jesus and prayed.
   (Kneel with hands in prayer position.)
But Jesus said, "There is work for you.
   (Reach out arms to comfort him.)
Don't ever be afraid!"
   (Shake head and smile.)

CALMING THE SEA

by Edith E. Cutting

WORDS	MOTIONS
Here is a boat On Galilee.	Hold hands together, shaping a boat.
Here are the waves On the stormy sea.	Move hands up and down over waves.
"Be still," said Jesus, And held out His hand.	Hold out hand in gesture of blessing.
Then the boat came quietly In to land.	Make boat again and move hands smoothly forward.

THE MAN FROM THE ROOF

by Edith E. Cutting

Four friends took one sick man to Jesus.
    (Hold up four fingers on one hand, one on the other.)
They carried him right on his bed.
    (Hold out arms, curved as if carrying.)
They couldn't get through all the people.
    (Turn this way and that, trying to find a way.)
They climbed up the stairway instead.
    (Step as if climbing stairs.)

They pulled a big hole in the roof top.
    (Reach down and throw away.)
It certainly didn't look neat!
    (Shake head.)
They lowered the man through the hole,
    (Arms in carrying position, lift, lower.)
And laid him by Jesus' feet.
    (Bend down to touch feet.)

"Get up," said Jesus to the man.
    (Reach out hand as if to help.)
"Get up and take your bed.
    (Lift hands as if to carry it on shoulder.)
Your sins are all forgiven you.
    (Reach hand out and up in gesture of benediction.)
Be well and good instead."
    (Two hands raised, then whole body bows in thanksgiving.)

FEEDING FIVE THOUSAND

by Edith E. Cutting

WORDS	MOTIONS
I had two little fish	Hold up two fingers.
And five rolls of bread.	Hold up five fingers on other hand.
I gave them to Jesus.	Reach out in giving gesture.
He blessed them,	Fold hands for prayer.
And 5,000 people were fed.	Spread arms wide.

GOD'S CARE
by Karin Glenn

Jesus taught the people. (Point up.)

He wanted them to know (Point to head.)

That God would take good care of them (Make arms outstretched.)

Because God loved them so. (Hug self.)

Jesus looked all about (Open hand above eyes, look around.)

And pointed to the sky, (Point to distant point.)

"I want you all to see the birds (Make circles with thumbs and index fingers, peer through.)

As they are flying by. (Flap arms.)

They don't store food for winter, (Shake head.)

But hungry they won't be. (Raise index finger, move from side to side.)

God will give them food to eat. (Peck with right fingers in left palm.)

God cares for them, you see. (Cup hands.)

And look at all the flowers (Make sweeping motion with arm.)

Nodding in the breeze. (Gently sway body from side to side.)

Does anyone have clothing (Touch shoulders with hands.)

More beautiful than these? (Move hands from shoulders and downward.)

But the flowers do not spin, (Make circle motion with hand.)

And flowers do not sew. (Make weaving motion with hand.)

It is God who dresses them, (Point up.)

That's what I want you to know. (Point to another.)

If God cares for the little birds (Flutter fingers.)

And all the flowers, too, (Put hands above head to form circle.)

Knowing that God loves you so (Hug self.)

Don't you think He'll care for you? (Point to another.)

So you need never worry (Shake head.)

About what to eat (point to mouth) or wear (Slide hands down front of body.)

For God is caring for you. (Spread arms wide.)

God's love is always there." (Hug self.)

GOD MADE ME

by Edith E. Cutting

This can be done by one child, or by a group with each one saying and demonstrating one line, or each saying one line and the whole group demonstrating.

WORDS	MOTIONS
God made my mouth.	Put finger to mouth.
God made my nose.	Put finger to nose.
God made my fingers.	Hold hands up and wiggle fingers.
God made my toes.	Bend over and touch toes.
God made my eyes	Put fingers to eyes.
So I can see.	Open eyes wide.
Aren't I wonderful?	Stretch arms wide and stand on tiptoe.
God made me!	Clasp hands over head and smile.

THANKSGIVING GIVING

by Edith E. Cutting

The group is lined up, each child holding one piece or can of food. They recite in unison:

Thank you, God,
For food to share   (Each holds up whatever he is carrying.)
With hungry people
Everywhere.

As each child carries his gift and places it on the altar or table, he says, "Thank you, God, for (apples, squash, bread, peas, turkey, etc.)," whichever one he is carrying.

When each has made his contribution, the group joins again in the benediction with hands in an attitude of prayer:

We thank you, God,
And now we pray
That no one goes hungry
On Thanksgiving Day.

This procedure can also be used as a class project making a poster collage, with each child pasting a picture of one kind of food on the poster.

FAMILIAR TUNES AND SONGS

FAMILIAR TUNES

SINGING WITH THE VERY YOUNG
   by Helen Kitchell Evans 26
WHAT DID THEY NAME THEIR CHILD?
   by Marcia Hornok 27
SAY, SAY, SAY YOUR PRAYERS
   by Virginia L. Kroll 28
TEN COMMANDMENTS
   by Virginia L. Kroll 28
HANNAH'S PRAYING
   by Virginia L. Kroll 28
CHRISTMAS CELEBRATION SONG
   by Marcia Hornok 29
MY SHEEP HEAR MY VOICE
   by Laura Cordova 30
JESUS LOVES YOU
   by Laura Cordova 30
READ, PRAY, GROW!
   by Laura Cordova 30
GOD MADE ME
   by Amy and Sarah Daniel 31
I'M A MIRACLE
   by Helen Kitchell Evans 31
NEW LIFE
   by Laura Cordova 32
FOLLOW THE SAVIOR
   by Laura Cordova 32
SING A SONG TO JESUS
   by Laura Cordova 32
SONG OF LOVE
   by Marcia Hornok 33
GOSPEL OF JOHN
   by Marcia Hornok 33
SPECIAL TO ME
   by Marcia Hornok 34
VALENTINE'S DAY
   by Marcia Hornok 34
STABLE SONG
   by Virginia L. Kroll 35
TELL-A-TALE
   by Virginia L. Kroll 35
THREE WISE MEN
   by Virginia L. Kroll 35
NOAH BUILDS A BOAT
   by Marilyn Senterfitt 36
BIBLE PEOPLE
   by Marilyn Senterfitt 36
AIN'T GONNA FIGHT NO MORE
   by Kathy Darling 37
I'D LIKE TO SING ABOUT MY DAD
   by Marcia Hornok 37
WHAT THE BELLS SAY
   by Helen Kitchell Evans 38
JESUS IS BORN
   by Helen Kitchell Evans 38
II PETER 1:2
   by Marcia Hornok 38
PRAYER BELLS
   by Kathy Darling 39
I'D LIKE TO THANK YOU
   by Kathy Darling 39
THE TWELVE DAYS OF CHRISTMAS
   by Marty Sharts 40
JESUS, OUR LORD AND SAVIOR
   by Laura Cordova 40
SETH'S SONG
   by Virginia L. Kroll 41
NOAH HAD A LITTLE DOVE
   by Virginia L. Kroll 41
WE LOVE YOU TODAY
   by Marcia Hornok 42
THANKSGIVING SONG
   by Marcia Hornok 42

SONGS

THREE CHEERS
   Words by Donna Colwell Rosser
   Music by Sandi Hess 43
MIRACLE OF LOVE
   Words and Music by Vickie J.
   Garrison 44
IT IS MARVELOUS
   Words and Music by Vickie J.
   Garrison 45
WHY SHOULD I WORRY
   Words and Music by Muriel
   Larson 46
KINDNESS
   Words and Music by Kathy
   Jones 46

SINGING WITH THE VERY YOUNG

by Helen Kitchell Evans

Singing with the very young is best learned by rote. Using a piano or other musical instrument enhances its pleasure. However, a pitch pipe may be used to guarantee the right pitch throughout the song.

Begin by reading aloud the words of the song to the children. Discuss the situation and background with the children, allowing them to contribute any ideas they might have. Help them to understand the meaning of the lyric so as to stir up the appropriate emotional setting.

The teacher should then sing the song, or sing and play as the children listen for the song, and note the spirit with which it is sung.

Next, the teacher should sing through the song with children joining in where they can. Following this step, it may be necessary to give special practice on those phrases where the time or melody have proven difficult.

The teacher should avoid singing the same song too often in a given day. Songs to be learned for a performance should be distributed through music periods for several weeks with concentration on them a few days before the presentation.

Teach children to stand straight and tall and to sing with high, sweet head-tones—tell them to sing "high in their head" like little birds singing their highest notes. *Never* tell children to "sing louder." This only brings out their "playground voices." These tones are certainly unpleasant when used in singing.

Also, group singing tends to stimulate some children to "show-off" or to attempt to dominate. The teacher must stress quality, not quantity of voice. Usually, the group settles down to better voice control and the end result is delightful—and sometimes amazing!

How songs are to be used depends on the nature of the lyric and its music. Usually, if the music is appealing, the words will follow and the children will beg to repeat the song, seeming never to tire.

WHAT DID THEY NAME THEIR CHILD?

by Marcia Hornok

Sung to: "The Bear Went over the Mountain"

Old Sarah had a new baby. Old Sarah had a new baby.
   Old Sarah had a new baby.
What did they name their child?
   They named him little ISAAC. They named him little ISAAC.
   They named him little ISAAC.
That's what they named their child.

When Hannah had a new baby, when Hannah had a new baby,
   When Hannah had a new baby,
What did they name their child?
   They named him little SAMUEL. They named him little SAMUEL.
   They named him little SAMUEL.
That's what they named their child.

E-lis-a-beth had a baby. E-lis-a-beth had a baby.
   E-lis-a-beth had a baby.
What did they name their child?
   They named him JO-HN, the Baptist. They named him JO-HN, the Baptist.
   They named him JO-HN, the Baptist.
That's what they named their child.

Young Mary had a new baby. Young Mary had a new baby.
   Young Mary had a new baby.
What did they name their child?
   They named Him SAVIOR, JESUS. They named Him SAVIOR, JESUS.
   They named Him SAVIOR, JESUS.
That's what they named their Child.

My Mother, too, had a baby. My Mother, too, had a baby.
   My Mother, too, had a baby.
What did they name their child?
   They named him/her _____ (child's name; if short, add "little" _____).
   They named him/her _____. They named him/her _____.
That's what they named their child.

CHORUS: That's what they named their child. That's what they named their child.
              They named him/her (little) _____.
              That's what they named their child.

SAY, SAY, SAY YOUR PRAYERS

by Virginia L. Kroll

Sung to: "Row, Row, Row Your Boat"

Say, say, say your prayers.
God is listening,
Under the blanket of night with the moon
And stars so glistening.

At morn when you wake,
Say them in the sun.
Jesus is with you to love and protect you
Until the day is done.

TEN COMMANDMENTS

by Virginia L. Kroll

Sung to: "Twinkle, Twinkle, Little Star"

Ten Commandments, what are they?
I'll explain them just this way:
Rules God did to people give
So they would know how to live.
Ten Commandments, sure and strong,
Teach me how to get along.

HANNAH'S PRAYING

by Virginia L. Kroll

Sung to: "Frere Jacques"

Hannah's praying, Hannah's praying,
Secretly,
Secretly;
Telling God her wishes,
Telling God her wishes,
Silently, silently.

What she wants most, what she wants most,
Is a boy,
Is a boy;
Samuel is her baby,
Samuel is her baby.
Oh what joy! Oh what joy!

CHRISTMAS CELEBRATION SONG

by Marcia Hornok

Sung to: "Oh You Can't Get to Heaven"

TEACHER:
Oh, we celebrate Christmas
With bells that ring.
'Cause bells that ring
Go ding-dong-ding.

CHILDREN:
Oh, we celebrate Christmas
With bells that ring.
'Cause bells that ring
Go ding-dong-ding.

EVERYONE: Oh, we celebrate Christmas with bells that ring,
'Cause bells that ring go ding-dong-ding.
And Jesus came
To earth that day.

Oh, we celebrate Christmas
With colored lights.
'Cause colored lights
Shine in the night.

Oh, we celebrate Christmas
With colored lights.
'Cause colored lights
Shine in the night.

EVERYONE: Oh, we celebrate Christmas with colored lights,
'Cause colored lights shine in the night.
And Jesus came
To earth that day.

Oh, we celebrate Christmas
With Christmas trees.
'Cause Christmas trees
Are sure to please.

Oh, we celebrate Christmas
With Christmas trees.
'Cause Christmas trees
Are sure to please.

EVERYONE: Oh, we celebrate Christmas with Christmas trees,
'Cause Christmas trees are sure to please.
And Jesus came
To earth that day.

(Children may think up other verses, even if they don't rhyme.)

MY SHEEP HEAR MY VOICE

by Laura Cordova

Sung to: "Oh How Lovely Is the Evening"

My sheep hear my voice and fo-ll-ow,
   Voice and fo-ll-ow.
I know them and they will fo-ll-ow,
   They will fo-ll-ow.
Follow Me. Follow Me.

JESUS LOVES YOU

by Laura Cordova

Sung to: "Frere Jacques"

Jesus loves you,
   Jesus loves you.
This I know,
   This I know.
He has given new life.
Saved us from the old life.
Praise the Lord! Praise the Lord!

READ, PRAY, GROW!

by Laura Cordova

Sung to: "Row, Row, Row Your Boat"

Read, read, read God's Word,
   Read it every day.
Happily, happily, happily, happily,
   Following God's way.

Pray, pray, pray to God,
   Pray at work or play.
Joyfully, joyfully, joyfully, joyfully,
   Pray to God each day.

Grow, grow, grow in the Lord,
   Stronger every day.
Merrily, merrily, merrily, merrily,
   Praise Him come what may.

GOD MADE ME

by Amy and Sarah Daniel

Sung to: "He's Got the Whole World in His Hands"

CHORUS: God made my whole body,
          Head to toe.
          God made my whole body,
          Head to toe.
          God made my whole body,
          Head to toe.
          God made my whole body,
          Head to toe.

Verse 1: God made every single hair,
          On my head.
          God made every single hair,
          On my head.
          God made every single hair,
          On my head.
          God made my whole body,
          Head to toe.

(Repeat 4th line of chorus for 4th line of each verse.)

Other verses might include:
- 2: God made both my eyes,
  And my nose, etc.
- 3: God made both my ears,
  And my mouth, etc.
- 4: God made my shoulders,
  And my neck, etc.
- 5: God made my two arms,
  And my hands, etc.
- 6: God made my ten fingers,
  And my wrists, etc.
- 7: God made my stomach,
  And my back, etc.
- 8: God made all my organs,
  And my skin, etc.
- 9: God made both my legs,
  And my feet, etc.
- 10: God made both my ankles,
  And ten toes, etc.

I'M A MIRACLE

by Helen Kitchell Evans

Sung to: "Rig-a-Jig-Jig"

God's miracles
Are wonderful,
Wonderful,
Wonderful.
God's miracles
Are wonderful,
For God made me,
You see.

I am a miracle,
Yes, sir-ee,
Oh, yes, sir-ee,
Oh, yes, sir-ee.
I am a miracle,
Yes, sir-ee,
God's miracle is me.

(Repeat above, replacing ME with YOU, I with YOU and AM with ARE.)
(Example: YOU are a miracle.)

He made our hands to
Wave this way,
Wave this way,
Wave this way.
He made our hands to
Wave this way.
We're miracles of God.

NEW LIFE

by Laura Cordova

Sung to: "The Muffin Man"

Have you met the Lord thy God,
 The Lord thy God,
 The Lord thy God?
Have you met the Lord thy God,
 Who is the King of Kings?

(Answer: Yes, I've met the Lord thy God.)

Have you trusted in the Lord,
 In the Lord,
 In the Lord?
Have you trusted in the Lord,
 For new life that He brings?

(Answer: Yes, I've trusted in the Lord.)

(Boys can ask the questions, and the girls can answer.)

FOLLOW THE SAVIOR

by Laura Cordova

Sung to: "Follow the Leader"

We're following the Savior,
 The Savior,
 The Savior.
We're following the Savior,
 Wherever He may go.

SING A SONG TO JESUS

by Laura Cordova

Sung to: "Sing a Song of Sixpence"

Sing a song to Jesus,
 Faces full of joy.
Hearts full of blessings
 For each girl and boy.

When you follow Jesus,
 Never should you stray;
But trust Him for your daily bread,
 And walk with Him each day.

SONG OF LOVE

by Marcia Hornok

Sung to: "Head, Shoulders, Knees and Toes"

I love Jesus, yes I do. Yes I do.
I love Jesus, yes I do. Yes I do-oo-oo-oo.
I love Jesus, and He loves me too.
I love Jesus, yes I do.

(Children's names can be substituted for the name, Jesus).

GOSPEL OF JOHN

by Marcia Hornok

Sung to: "Frere Jacques"

This song will acquaint children with the contents of the first four chapters of the Gospel of John. Children can hold up the appropriate number of fingers when they sing the last line of each verse.

Children repeat each line after the teacher until the song is known well enough to use variations, such as boys echoing girls or whispering the repeated lines.

TEACHER	CHILDREN
John the Baptist Saw God's Son; He's the One to follow. Chapter one.	John the Baptist Saw God's Son; He's the One to follow. Chapter one.
At a wedding, Jesus knew Miracles were needed. Chapter two.	At a wedding, Jesus knew Miracles were needed. Chapter two.
Nicodemus, Verily You must be reborn. Chapter three.	Nicodemus, Verily You must be reborn. Chapter three.
Needy woman, Thirst no more. Jesus is the answer. Chapter four.	Needy woman, Thirst no more. Jesus is the answer. Chapter four.
He will help me, When I pray, For my needs and problems, Every day.	He will help me, When I pray, For my needs and problems, Every day.

SPECIAL TO ME

by Marcia Hornok

Sung to: "My Bonnie Lies over the Ocean"

My Jesus is great, and I love Him.
My Jesus is special to me.
My Jesus is great, and I love Him.
I'll always love Jesus, you see.

Jesus, Jesus, I'll always love Jesus, you see, you see.
Jesus, Jesus, my Jesus is special to me.

Substitute the following for *Jesus*: Mommy, Daddy, Grandpa, Grandma, teacher, sister, brother, pastor, etc.

VALENTINE'S DAY

by Marcia Hornok

Sung to: "The Farmer in the Dell"

Note: Children can sing this song while passing out their valentines to each other, or it can be sung as a game with all children holding hands to form a big circle. One child in the middle chooses another child from the circle, and that child chooses the next, and so on. If the children are able, they can walk in a circle while singing.

A valentine for you.
A valentine for you.
Be-cause I love you so,
A valentine for you.

A happy wish for you.
A happy wish for you.
Be-cause I love you so,
A happy wish for you.

A friendly smile for you.
A friendly smile for you.
Be-cause I love you so,
A friendly smile for you.

(Repeat verses until all children have been chosen.)

STABLE SONG

by Virginia L. Kroll

Sung to: "Rock-A-Bye, Baby"

Rock-a-bye, Jesus, in a cow's stall
With hay for the floor and wood for the wall.
When You are present,
Any old place
Turns into a temple
Full of Your grace.

TELL-A-TALE

by Virginia L. Kroll

Recited to the meter of: "Pat-a-Cake, Pat-a-Cake, Baker's Man"

Tell-a-tale, tell-a-tale, if you can.
Mine is about a servant man.
He wears no crown, nor robe, nor ring,
But He's the most important King.

Guess His name, guess His name, if you can.
He's really God born as a man.
If you said "Jesus," you are right,
Jesus the Savior and the Light.

THREE WISE MEN

by Virginia L. Kroll

Sung to: "Three Blind Mice"

Three wise men, three wise men,
See how they come,
See how they come.
They followed the Star where the Baby lay.
They knelt with the animals in the hay.
They worshiped the King and went on their way,
The three wise men.

NOAH BUILDS A BOAT

by Marilyn Senterfitt

Sung to: "Mary Had a Little Lamb"

1
Noah one day heard God speak,
Heard God speak, heard God speak.
Noah one day heard God speak.
Noah was humbly meek.

2
God said, "Noah build a boat,
Build a boat, build a boat."
God said, "Noah build a boat,
And be sure it will float."

3
"Put the pairs of animals in,
Animals in, animals in.
Put the pairs of animals in,
Each fur, feather and fin."

4
Noah quickly obeyed God's call,
Obeyed God's call, obeyed God's call.
Noah quickly obeyed God's call;
Built a boat strong and tall.

5
Animals went in two by two,
Two by two, two by two.
Animals went in two by two;
Noah's family went, too.

6
The sky opened and rain came down,
Rain came down, rain came down.
The sky opened and rain came down.
The boat was safe and sound.

BIBLE PEOPLE

by Marilyn Senterfitt

Sung to: "Old MacDonald Had a Farm"

1
Abraham, Isaac, Jacob:
Patriarchs were they.
Samson, Gideon, Deborah:
Wise judges were they.
With a Bible here
And a Bible there;
Your Bible, my Bible,
Everywhere a Bible.
Read the word of God each day
To learn about them.

2
David, Solomon, Ahab:
Regal kings were they.
Elijah, Jonah, Amos:
All prophets were they.
With a Bible here
And a Bible there;
Your Bible, my Bible,
Everywhere a Bible.
Read the word of God each day
To learn about them.

3
Simon Peter, Andrew, John:
Disciples were they.
Jesus Christ the Son of God:
The Saviour is He.
With a Bible here
And a Bible there;
Your Bible, my Bible,
Everywhere a Bible.
Read the word of God each day
To learn about them.

AIN'T GONNA FIGHT NO MORE

by Kathy Darling

Sung to: "It Ain't Gonna Rain No More"

I ain't gonna fight no more, no more.
I ain't gonna fight no more.
When I play I'll share my toy.
I ain't gonna fight no more.

I ain't gonna push no more, no more.
I ain't gonna push no more.
When I play I'll take my turn.
I ain't gonna push no more!

I ain't gonna grab no more, no more.
I ain't gonna grab no more.
When I play I'll be polite.
I ain't gonna grab no more.

Help me play, my Lord, my Lord.
Help me play, my Lord.
Teach me how to be a friend,
And I'll have fun, my Lord.

I'D LIKE TO SING ABOUT MY DAD

by Marcia Hornok

Sung to: "I'd Like to Teach the World to Sing"

I'd like to sing about my Dad, he's really someone swell.
His love for me and fam-i-ly is what I'm proud to tell.
I know I'm safe within his care, and he provides for me.
He makes our home a happy place. That's where I want to be.

Chorus:
   He is really great.
   There is no debate.
   I anticipate . . .
   Him I'll imitate.

Remember when you got your tools? I saw them hanging there.
The next time when you needed them, they were scattered everywhere.
At night when you come home from work, and need a little rest,
You lie there sleeping on the couch, then I jump up on your chest.

Repeat Chorus

WHAT THE BELLS SAY

by Helen Kitchell Evans

Sung to: "Hickory Dickory Dock"

Church bells are ringing today.
What do those church bells say?
They say that Easter time is here,
The season we all hold dear.

JESUS IS BORN

by Helen Kitchell Evans

Sung to: "Frere Jacques"

And she brought forth,
Yes, she brought forth,
Her dear son,
Her dear son.
Placed him in a manger;
Shielded him from danger,
Her first son,
Her first son.

In that country,
In that country,
In a field,
In a field,
Shepherds stood by watching,
Shepherds stood by watching,
Through the night,
Through the night.

Lo the angel
Of the Lord came
Down to earth,
Down to earth.
Glory shone around them,
Brightly shone around them.
They were afraid.
They were afraid.

Then the angel
Said unto them,
"What you see
Was foretold.
Now I bring glad tidings,
Tidings to all people.
Fear not, shepherds
Behold."

In the city
Known as David,
Jesus Christ is now born.
Peace on earth to all men.
Glory in the highest.
Christ is born,
Christ is born.

II PETER 1:2

by Marcia Hornok

Sung to: "Oh, My Darlin' Clementine"

Grace and peace be multiplied, multiplied unto you,
Through the knowledge of God, and of Jesus, our Lord.
Grace and peace be multiplied, multiplied unto you,
Through the knowledge of God, and of Jesus, our Lord.

II Peter 1:2

PRAYER BELLS

by Kathy Darling

Sung to: "London Bridge Is Falling Down"

Prayer bells are ringing loud, ringing loud, ringing loud.

Prayer bells are ringing loud. Praise you, Jesus!

Candles tall are glowing bright, glowing bright, glowing bright.

Candles tall are glowing bright. Praise you, Jesus!

Voices high are singing sweet, singing sweet, singing sweet.

Voices high are singing sweet. Praise you, Jesus!

Hearts and hands we give to you, give to you, give to you.

Hearts and hands we give to you. Praise you, Jesus!

I'D LIKE TO THANK YOU

by Kathy Darling

Sung to: "Michael Row the Boat Ashore"

Lord, I'd like to thank you now, alleluia!
Lord, I'd like to thank you now, alleluia!

Lord, you gave me family, alleluia!
Lord, you gave my friends to me, alleluia!

For the fish and birds of air, alleluia!
For the beasts and growling bear, alleluia!

Lord, I'd like to thank you now, alleluia!
For the trees and sky and land, alleluia!

THE TWELVE DAYS OF CHRISTMAS

by Marty Sharts

Sung to: "Twelve Days of Christmas"

On the first day of Christmas my Jesus gave to me, a lesson to live by.

On the second day of Christmas my Jesus gave to me, the Christmas star.

On the third day of Christmas my Jesus gave to me, three wise men.

On the fourth day of Christmas my Jesus gave to me, joy everywhere.

On the fifth day of Christmas my Jesus gave to me, all of God's love.

On the sixth day of Christmas my Jesus gave to me, hope for salvation.

On the seventh day of Christmas my Jesus gave to me, seven angels singing.

On the eighth day of Christmas my Jesus gave to me, eight stars shining.

On the ninth day of Christmas my Jesus gave to me, nine snowflakes falling.

On the tenth day of Christmas my Jesus gave to me, ten shepherds praying.

On the eleventh day of Christmas my Jesus gave to me, eleven candles glowing.

On the twelfth day of Christmas my Jesus gave to me, twelve choirs singing.

JESUS, OUR LORD AND SAVIOR

by Laura Cordova

Sung to: "Rudolph the Red-Nosed Reindeer"

Jesus, our Lord and Savior,
   Came to us on Christmas Day.
And if you love the Savior,
   You will follow in His way.

All of the rooms were taken
   There was no room in the inn.
They wouldn't let poor Mary,
   Find a place to rest within.

On that starry Christmas Day,
   Jesus came to earth.
Angels and the Shepherds came
   To celebrate His birth.

Oh how the children love Him;
   He takes each one upon His knee.
Because all His precious children,
   Will live with Him eternally.

SETH'S SONG

by Virginia L. Kroll

Sung to: "Frere Jacques"

Cain and Abel
Are my brothers.
How they fight!
How they fight!
Breaking up the family,
Breaking up the family,
It's not right,
It's not right.

Families should
Love each other.
That's God's way,
That's God's way;
Helping one another,
Helping one another,
Every day,
Every day.

NOAH HAD A LITTLE DOVE

by Virginia L. Kroll

Sung to: "Mary Had a Little Lamb"

Noah had a little dove, little dove, little dove.
Noah had a little dove
With feathers white as snow.

He sent the dove to fly away, fly away, fly away.
He sent the dove to fly away;
Far from him it did go.

The dove came back; it had no branch, had no branch, had no branch.
The dove came back; it had no branch,
And Noah's head hung low.

He sent the white dove out again, out again, out again.
He sent the white dove out again;
His faith did ever grow.

It brought him back a leafy twig, leafy twig, leafy twig.
It brought him back a leafy twig;
How Noah's face did glow!

WE LOVE YOU TODAY

by Marcia Hornok

Sung to: "Happy Birthday to You"

We love _____ today.   We love _____ today.
          child's name   child's name

God bless _____, we pray.
             child's name

Help him/her have a good day.

After singing "Happy Birthday" to a child, this verse can be added, or this verse can be sung to various children, just to show love even when it's not their birthday.

THANKSGIVING SONG

by Marcia Hornok

Sung to: "London Bridge Is Falling Down"

Thank you for the food we eat, food we eat, food we eat.
Thank you for the food we eat.
We're so thankful.

Thank you for the clothes we wear, clothes we wear, clothes we wear.
Thank you for the clothes we wear.
We're so thankful.

Thank you that we're growing strong, growing strong, growing strong.
Thank you that we're growing strong.
We're so thankful.

Thank you that we're in this school, in this school, in this school.
Thank you that we're in this school.
We're so thankful.

Thank you for the friends we love, friends we love, friends we love.
Thank you for the friends we love.
We're so thankful.

Thank you Jesus for Your love, for Your love, for Your love.
Thank you Jesus for Your love.
We're so thankful.

(Children may be able to think of other things to sing about.)

4. Three cheers for sunny skies.
   Three cheers for hopes held high.
   Three cheers for sunny skies to hold our hopes up high.
   (chorus)

5. Three cheers for happy hearts.
   Three cheers for smiles to start.
   Three cheers for happy hearts where happy smiles can start.
   (chorus)

CHORAL READINGS AND PANTOMIMES

RHYTHM AND MOTION
  by Helen Kitchell Evans 48
LIFE OF SAMUEL
  by Marcia Hornok 49
OBEY YOUR PARENTS
  by Marcia Hornok 50
SPECIAL THINGS
  by Helen Kitchell Evans 51
THE BIRTH OF A KING
  by Helen Kitchell Evans 51
THANKSGIVING PROGRAM
  by Marcia Hornok 52
BIBLE RAP
  by Lenore Kruz 53
A GARDEN
  by Edith E. Cutting 53
EASTER IS HERE
  by Helen Kitchell Evans 54
EASTER DAY
  by Helen Kitchell Evans 54
WONDERFUL, WONDERFUL CHRISTMAS!
  by Helen Kitchell Evans 55
FILLED WITH LOVE
  by Helen Kitchell Evans 55
BLESSED CHRISTMAS DAY
  by Helen Kitchell Evans 56
TIME FOR HAPPINESS
  by Helen Kitchell Evans 56
HEALING THE CRIPPLED WOMAN
  by Edith E. Cutting 57
OUR SAVIOR
  by Laura Cordova 57
THE SOWER
  by Laura Cordova 58
THE LEAST OF THESE
  by Laura Cordova 59
THE FIG TREE
  by Laura Cordova 60
THE LOST COIN
  by Laura Cordova 60

RHYTHM AND MOTION
by Helen Kitchell Evans

The sections of choral readings and pantomimes in this book were chosen because of their rhythm and suitability for responsive reading and moving.

The younger children only beginning their experience with choral readings and pantomimes need to hear the selections read by a teacher or parent. The selection should be read two or three times before an attempt is made to speak in unison or make appropriate movements.

Where the material to be spoken is more than a simple refrain, it should be talked about. The adult should give the children the interpretation of key phrases and sentences. This discussion should include:
  1. Highly meaningful words
  2. Places where tempo is speeded up or slowed down
  3. Places where pauses should or should not come

After this discussion, the teacher should again read the selection, allowing the children to chime in at will. Lines or phrases that prove to be more difficult may need separate work.

A choral reading that has two groups who alternate "speeches" is more difficult, but little ones can learn simple selections and thoroughly enjoy this type of choral reading.

The grouping may be girls and boys, left and right half of pupil group, or pupils with high-pitched and low-pitched voices.

The teacher may need to "speak" along with any group that tends to become sing-song.

Suggestions for help:
  1. Keep the child's mind on the meaning of the selection.
  2. Write on the chalkboard the word or phrase from each line that has the most meaning. Point to those words as the selection is read.
  3. Encourage the child to bring out the meaning as he/she recites.
  4. Show them how to break the habit of stopping at the end of a line if the meaning continues in the following line.

If the recitations and choral readings are to be presented before an audience, they should be thoroughly memorized. Psychology teaches us that the whole-method of memorization is preferable. Encourage the children to listen to the entire selection. Then have each child concentrate on the part to which he/she has been assigned. Repetition from an older member of the child's family may be helpful.

These choral readings and poems may be used for fun and appreciation, as well as for public performance. Engaging in choral speech work is most enjoyable, and the children who are blessed with a teacher who loves this form of expression are most fortunate.

LIFE OF SAMUEL

by Marcia Hornok

Older children: "Hannah praying for a son,
　　　　　　　And God gave her one."

Youngest children are in crouched position. They rise slowly, reaching arms in air as they stand, while all children say,
　　　"See Samuel growing."

Older children: "Samuel and his family bow
　　　　　　　At the temple now."

Several children bow on knees with hands folded in prayer and head bowed, while all children say:
　　　"See Samuel worship."

Older children: "Samuel helping Priest Eli
　　　　　　　Tells his Mom, 'Good-bye.'"
All children wave.

All children:　"See Samuel working."

　One child carries a trash basket across stage.
　One child pushes a broom across stage.
　One child sets a candle on a table.
　One child sets dishes on a table.
　One child places a pitcher on the table.
　One child shakes a carpet and lays it down.
　Etc.

Older children: "Hannah sewing with great care
　　　　　　　　Coats for Samuel to wear."
　One child wearing a simple coat or bathrobe, steps forward, extends arms, and makes a complete circle, modeling the coat.

All children:　"See Samuel sleeping."
　All children place head on back of clasped hands, tilt head to side, and close eyes.

OBEY YOUR PARENTS

by Marcia Hornok

Have older children on one side of choir and younger children on the other. Children can hold pictures they have made of their families, either hand-drawn or cut from catalogs.

ALL: Children.

OLDER: Obey your parents in the Lord.

YOUNGER: For this is right.

GIRLS: Yes, Mother.

BOYS: Right away, Father.

ALL: For this is right.

OLDER: Working   YOUNGER: Together
Playing   Together
Singing   Together
Praying   Together

Riding   Together
Caring   Together
Reading   Together
Sharing   Together

Laughing   Together
Walking   Together
Crying   Together
Talking   Together

But . . . always . . .   (loud) Together.

ALL: For this is right.

OLDER: Honor your father and mother, that it may be well with you.

GIRLS: Daddy, you are wonderful.

BOYS: Mommy, we sure love you.

OLDER: We want to please you.

YOUNGER: And do our best.

ALL: For this is right.

SPECIAL THINGS

by Helen Kitchell Evans

First child:
: Good foods, a lovely tree,
Gifts and special things;

Second child:
: These are some joys
That every Christmas brings.

Third child:
: A time to be with family,
Good friends get together;

Fourth child:
: All enjoy Christmas
Regardless of the weather.

All four:
: Goodwill is everywhere,
Peace comes to everyone,
For on this special day
God gave to us His Son.

THE BIRTH OF A KING

by Helen Kitchell Evans

Choir 1:
: No room was prepared
In splendid array.

Choir 2:
: No quilts or satins,
Just sweet-smelling hay.

Solo 1:
: No tapes played music
To soothe Him to sleep.

Solo 2:
: Only Mary's soft voice
And the baa-ing of sheep.

Chorus:
: No TV announcement
Yet the news spread like a flame;
Many traveled for miles
The night Jesus came.

Solo 3:
: The events of that night
Sweet memories bring

Chorus:
: It gave us our Savior
Our Lord and our King!

THANKSGIVING PROGRAM

by Marcia Hornok

Children recite the four main lines in unison. Between each line, individual children say what they're thankful for.

All: WE THANK GOD FOR HIS BLESSINGS:
Child wearing sunglasses: "Thank you for the sunshine."
Child holding dog leash: "Thank you for the animals."
Child holding Bible: "Thank you for the Bible."
Child making swimming motions: "Thank you for swimming pools."
Child holding flowers: "Thank you for the flowers."
Child rubbing tummy: "Thank you for happy feelings."
Child holding framed picture of his family: "Thank you for our families."
Child hugging himself: "Thank you for loving us."

All: WE THANK OUR PARENTS, TOO:
Children hold pictures they have drawn of the item they give thanks for:
"Thank you for our house."
"Thank you for my toys."
"Thank you for good meals."
"Thank you for reading to me."
"Thank you for brothers and sisters."
"Thank you for vacations."
"Thank you for picnics."
"Thank you for taking us places."

All: WE THANK THE ONES WHO HELP US:
"Thank you, Mr. Policeman."
"Thank you, Doctors and Nurses."
"Thank you, Pastor _____." (Use name, if appropriate.)
"Thank you, President _____."
"Thank you, Governor _____."
"Thank you, Grandma and Grandpa."
"Thank you, _____." (Use teacher's name.)

All: 'CAUSE THANKING'S FUN TO DO.

Everyone says, "Thank you very much" together and makes a bow or curtsy.

Note: Children can be encouraged to think up the things they are thankful for and use these in the program in place of some things listed.

BIBLE RAP

by Lenore Kruz

ALL: We're here to tell you about the Bible.
SOLO: To follow Jesus and be a disciple.
SOLO: He preached to 5000, now that was a bunch.
SOLO: But when He was finished, they said:
ALL: What's for lunch?
SOLO: Up stepped a boy who knew the score.
ALL: Said I brought my lunch, nothing more!
SOLO: He had two fishes and five loaves of bread.
ALL: That's all Jesus needed, He did the rest.

ALL: Said the bride to the groom, "we're in a stew;
SOLO: We've run out of wine, what will we do?"
SOLO: Mary said, "My son, can do it!"
ALL: With Jesus' help, there's nothing to it.

SOLO: Now Thomas was a doubter, he didn't believe,
ALL: Then he saw those wounds when Jesus rolled up His sleeve.
ALL: He healed the sick and He raised the dead.
ALL: He fed 5000 on fish and bread.

SOLO: Now what these folks all need you see
ALL: Is faith my friend, like you and me.
SOLO: Yes faith my friend, no need to fuss.
ALL: We're all His lambs. He cares for us!

A GARDEN

by Edith E. Cutting

This may be done so that the teacher gives each child a package of seeds after the verse is said, or the children may be messengers to distribute packages of seeds to members of the congregation.

Child 1: We're going to plant a garden.
Child 2: And see God make it grow.
Child 3: He will send the sunshine and rain.
Child 4: And these are the seeds to sow.

EASTER IS HERE

by Helen Kitchell Evans

Child 1:	Happy day of Resurrection!
Joyful Easter Day!
We're so glad you came
To worship and to pray.

Child 2:	Let us sing
In joyful praise;
Easter is
The day of days!

All:	"A Happy Day" (Rhythm: "Jack, Be Nimble")

Let us worship,
Let us pray;
Easter is such
A happy day.

Child 3:	Just because I'm little
Don't think for one minute
That I can't enjoy Easter—
I know the joy that's in it!

Child 4:	I love Jesus so much
I'll stand up here and say:
He leads me where I go
On Easter and every day.

Child 5:	I suppose because I'm three
They gave two lines to me.

Anyway—Bye—Happy Easter!

EASTER DAY

by Helen Kitchell Evans

Child 1:	Jesus said, "I'll go away,
I'll come again
Another day."

Child 2:	Angels rolled
The stone away,
On Easter Day,
On Easter Day.

Child 3:	Up in Heaven
Jesus lives
With the Father
Who forgives.

Child 4:	Flowers bloom
Because it's Spring,
Giving joy
To everything.

Child 5:	I'm as happy
As can be;
Jesus lives,
He lives for me.

WONDERFUL, WONDERFUL CHRISTMAS!

by Helen Kitchell Evans

Chorus:	Wonderful, wonderful Christmas!
Solo 1:	The birthday of our King;
Solo 2:	The Son of God sent down to earth,
Solo 3:	Let's rejoice and sing!
Chorus:	Wonderful, wonderful Christmas!
Solo 4:	Glorious day filled with cheer;
Solo 5:	When we celebrate with our Savior
	At this season every year.
Chorus:	Wonderful, wonderful Christmas!
Solo 6:	Oh, how we love this season;
Solo 7:	God seems so extra close to us
	That truly is the reason.
Chorus:	Wonderful, wonderful Christmas!

FILLED WITH LOVE

by Helen Kitchell Evans

Group 1:	Our arms are the manger, (Fold arms to form manger.) Filled with heavenly light;
Group 2:	Our hearts are the shepherd's fold (Place hands over heart.) Where angels came that night;
Both groups:	We're filled with the love of Jesus (Put both hands out, look up.)
	The thoughts of that wonderful day, (Touch head with both hands.)
	When little Baby Jesus Slept on a bed of hay. (Fold arms to form manger.)

BLESSED CHRISTMAS DAY

by Helen Kitchell Evans

First child: Christmas is more than lights,

Second child: Christmas is more than trees;

Third child: Christmas is more than joy
With gifts we hope will please.

Fourth child: Christmas is more than stockings
Hung up for you and me;

Fifth child: Christmas is more than candy
For Christmas is love, you see.

Sixth child: Christmas is love for the Christ Child
Born on a bed of hay;

Seventh child: A Child sent to save the world,
So let's worship and always pray.

Eighth child: Let's never forget the blessings,
God sends to us each day.

Ninth child: Let's never forget God's love
He's good to us in every way.

All: Thank you, Heavenly Father,
For this blessed Christmas Day.

TIME FOR HAPPINESS

by Helen Kitchell Evans

Child 1: It's time to be happy.

Child 2: It's time to be glad.

Child 3: It's time to be cheerful.

Child 4: No one should be sad.

Child 1: For this is the day
That our Savior came;

Child 2: He made all of us brothers,

Child 3: He loved all the same.

Child 4: Christmas is lovely,
The day of His birth;

All: The day that salvation
Came for all on this earth.

HEALING THE CRIPPLED WOMAN

by Edith E. Cutting

WORDS	MOTIONS
A poor old woman's Back was sore	Place hands on back with face ready to cry.
And so bent she could only Look at the floor.	Bend way over with hand still on sore back.
She came to Jesus When she heard His call. He healed her and made her straight and tall.	Walk with head still down, body bent. Put hand to ear, listening. Stand straight, smile, and lift arms up to be as tall as possible.

OUR SAVIOR

by Laura Cordova

Props:
Using large pieces of poster board, write each letter for the word S A V I O R. Have the children stand, holding their letter cards, with their backs toward the audience. As each one completes his/her verse, the next one turns around and says his/hers.

S — is the Savior, born on Christmas Day.

A — is for angels, telling the way.

V — is for victory, victory from sin.

I — is for into, won't you let Him come in?

O — is for only, He is the only way.

R — is for rejoice, it's Christmas Day!

THE SOWER

by Laura Cordova

To do this action parable, have a narrator read each verse as the children pantomime actions.

Narrator:

Behold, a sower went out to sow.	(Pretend to cast seed from an imaginary pouch.)
And as he sowed, some seed fell by the wayside; and the birds came and devoured them.	(Walk around flapping arms like wings and pretending to eat seeds.)
Some fell on stony places, where they did not have much earth; and they immediately sprang up because they had no depth of earth.	(Crouch down low, then spring up with hands out stretched like little leaves.)
But when the sun was up they were scorched, and because they had no root they withered away.	(Droop hands and slowly "wither" down.)
And some fell among thorns, and the thorns sprang up and choked them.	(Children pretend to choke little plants.)
But others fell on good ground and yielded a crop: some a hundredfold, some sixty, some thirty.	(Slowly reach up higher and higher.)
But he who received seed on the good ground is he who hears the word and understands it, who indeed bears fruit and produces: some a hundredfold, some sixty, some thirty.	(Children pretend to hold open Bibles in their hands, and nod and smile as if they understand and receive it.)

THE LEAST OF THESE

by Laura Cordova

Based on Matthew 25:31-46

Cast: Narrator and 6 children.

Props: Fruit, a cup, sweater and flowers.

Narrator:
Then the King will say to those on His right hand, "Come, you blessed of My Father, inherit the kingdom prepared for you from the foundation of the world."

Narrator:

For I was hungry and you gave me food;	(First child hands an apple or other fruit to the second child.)
I was thirsty and you gave me drink;	(Second child hands a cup to third child.)
I was a stranger and you took me in.	(Third child shakes hands with fourth child.)
I was naked and you clothed me.	(Fourth child hands sweater to fifth child.)
I was sick and you visited me . . .;	(Fifth child hands flowers to sixth child.)

Then the righteous will answer Him saying, "Lord, when did we see You hungry and feed you, or thirsty and give you drink? When did we see you a stranger and take you in, or naked and clothed you? Or when did we see you sick or in prison and come to you?"

And the King will answer and say to them, "Assuredly, I say to you, in as much as you did it to one of the least of these my brethren, you did it to me."

THE FIG TREE

by Laura Cordova

Based on Luke 13:6-9

Narrator:

A certain man had a fig tree planted in his vineyard, and he came seeking fruit on it and found none. (Children pretend to look for fruit on a tree, but can't find any and shake their heads.)

Then he said to the keeper of the vineyard, "Look, for three years I have come seeking fruit on this fig tree and find none. Cut it down; why does it use up the ground?" (Look cross and shake finger as though scolding.)

But the keeper of the vineyard answered and said to him, "Sir, let it alone this year also, until I dig around it and fertilize it. (Pretend to dig around tree.)

And if it bears fruit, well. But if not, after that you can cut it down." (Pretend to chop down tree with an axe.)

Every tree that does not bear good fruit is cut down and thrown into the fire. Therefore, by their fruits you will know them. (Pretend to pick up tree and carry it away.)

THE LOST COIN

by Laura Cordova

Cast: Girl and her friends, two boys.

Props: A coin, chair, small table and a lamp.

A girl sits down on the chair. She reaches into her pocket to take out a coin, but finds it is lost! She looks around, but can't find it. Next she pretends to turn on the lamp and look around, but still can't find it. Finally she picks up a broom and begins to sweep the room and finds the lost coin under the chair. A big smile comes over her face, and she waves for her friends to come see her coin. They all walk away happily.

Two more children walk up to the front. One is carrying an open Bible. He points to different passages and the other nods in agreement. They kneel down as though praying together.

Read Verse:
"Likewise, I say unto you, there is joy in the presence of the angels of God over one sinner that repenteth" (Luke 15:8-10).

SKITS AND PLAYS

ACT IT OUT!
　by Helen Kitchell Evans 62
GOD'S BEAUTIFUL WORLD
　by Marilyn Senterfitt 63
DAVID AND HIS SHEEP
　by Marilyn Senterfitt 65
A GOOD MAN
　by Marion Schoeberlein 66
GO, JESUS. OBEY YOUR FATHER.
　by Catherine Deverell 67
THE SAD SISTERS
　by Katherine D.M. Marko 69
THE GIANT
　by Marion Schoeberlein 71
WHERE YOU GO
　by Katherine D.M. Marko 72
SAUL WAS HIS NAME
　by Katherine D.M. Marko 73
THE ROCK THAT FOLLOWED THEM
　by Laura Cordova 75
A SON COMES HOME
　by Marilyn Senterfitt 77
THE TREES CHOOSE A KING
　by Marilyn Senterfitt 79
MOSES CHOSEN
　by Virginia L. Kroll 81
THE MAN IN THE TREE
　by Marion Schoeberlein 82
NOAH AND HIS NEIGHBORS
　by Virginia L. Kroll 83
LOST AND FOUND
　by Clara Burton Smith 85
THE LADY WHO TURNED INTO SALT
　by Marion Schoeberlein 88
MARY AND MARTHA
　by Marion Schoeberlein 89
MARY'S ANGEL
　by Marion Schoeberlein 90
THE CAMELS AND THE CHRISTMAS PLAY
　by Virginia Hoppes 91
WE TRUST IN GOD
　by Ellen Javernick 93
CHRISTMAS FINALE
　by Helen Kitchell Evans 95

Shining Star Publications, Copyright © 1990, A division of Good Apple, Inc.

ACT IT OUT!

by Helen Kitchell Evans

Acting is for everyone! Some children naturally like to entertain a group. Others are shy and awkward (or they think they are). These are children who have never had an opportunity to do simple acting.

Before the teacher uses the material in this book, he/she may wish to start with a game, a group stunt, or a tableau in which anyone can take part. It is such a good way to have fun together.

Since most of the very young desire to be a part of plays and performances, the use of a narrator often gives the teacher an opportunity to include many children. The narrator is used especially well to present the text of the play with children pantomiming or presenting group scenes.

The plays in this book may be presented as shown. Or, the teacher may read a play aloud, then allow the children to act the play or manipulate puppets using their own words.

It is the purpose of plays experienced at this early age to give meaning to the word drama. Some children seem to have no creative ability, but simple plays with simple actions develop this ability. When the "ice is broken," the children's natural bent toward playacting is likely to emerge.

These little plays need few, if any, stage props. A draped chair becomes a throne; a long dress and a wig transforms a three-year-old into (in her words) an "old lady."

At this age spontaneous reaction to a dramatic situation is preferable. We see emotional responses, a flow of language, and natural gestures developing and beginning to emerge. The skillful teacher will utilize these plays in this book in such a way as to contribute the most to her pupil's development.

> So let's begin
> And act it out!
> We'll have fun
> Without a doubt.

Note to teachers: Very young children are able to take part in the little plays in this book. The secret for them is to remember which of their friends speaks just before they do. Thus, many children may be on stage and yet have only one or two lines of script to remember.

GOD'S BEAUTIFUL WORLD

by Marilyn Senterfitt

OBJECTIVE: To help younger children understand the wondrous miracle of God's creation. Children will benefit by helping to make the props.

MATERIALS: You will need heavy paper or poster board, pictures of plants, fish and animals, and either an easel to hold the poster board, or else a small bulletin board.

CAST: Narrator may be an older child, youth or adult. Twelve or more children may participate.

PROPS: Cut out a large white circle (all circles should be the same size). Color, paint or glue black paper on opposite side. Cut half circles of light blue and dark blue. Cut brown piece as shown in illustration. Make other circles of bright yellow, light yellow, and several more white circles. On six white circles draw or glue pictures of trees, flowers, birds, fish, and animals, and cover one with large stars. Circles represent the following:

    Black/White—darkness and light
    Light-blue half—sky
    Dark-blue half—water
    Brown piece—land
    Bright yellow—sun
    Light yellow—moon
    White—stars, plants, trees, fish, birds, animals

SETTING THE SCENE: Place easel at child's level with poster or bulletin board stage in the center. Narrator stands to right or left. Two leaders may assist children by handing each their circle and directing them on stage. Children with black/white, light-blue half, brown piece, bright yellow and half of plants, trees, fish, etc., enter stage left. From stage right the children with the dark-blue half, light yellow, stars and remaining plants, trees, fish, etc., may enter. Attach large loops of tape to back of sky, water and land pieces so that they will hold to white circle as shown.

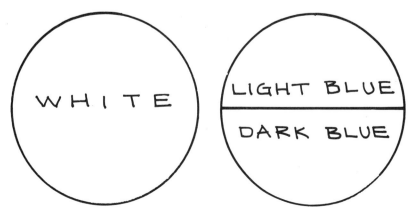

NARRATOR: Long ago there was only God and a great blackness.
(*Child with black circle enters stage left, stands stage center, and holds it up.*)

NARRATOR: Then God decided to change all that. He commanded, "Let there be light," and light appeared.
(*Child turns over circle showing white side. Places on easel and exits stage left.*)

NARRATOR: God was now ready to make the blue skies.
(*Child enters stage right and attaches light blue at top of circle. Exits stage left.*)

NARRATOR: And the dark-blue waters below.
(*Child enters stage right and attaches dark-blue half at bottom. Exits stage right.*)

NARRATOR: Then God placed rich brown land in the dark-blue waters.
(*Child enters stage left and places brown piece on blue water. Exits stage left.*)

NARRATOR: All of this was very good but God had only just begun. He next covered the land with green grass, plants, trees and beautiful flowers.
(*Children enter both stage right and left, stand on either side of easel and hold circles up showing the plants, trees, etc. They remain on stage.*)

NARRATOR: God saw that the land was now beautiful but the sky above was bare. God put the warm yellow sun in the daytime sky.
(*Child enters stage left and stands among the plants, etc.*)

NARRATOR: And at night He placed a bright moon and millions of stars.
(*Moon and stars enter stage right and stand among plants, etc.*)

NARRATOR: God was very pleased, but He was not finished. In the dark-blue waters, God placed all kinds of fish.
(*Fish enter stage left and right and join other children.*)

NARRATOR: In the skies, birds flew and sang.
(*Birds enter stage left and right.*)

NARRATOR: And on the land He placed wondrous animals of all kinds.
(*Animals enter stage left and right.*)

NARRATOR: God had one last thing to make. This would be the most special of all. God made something to take care of His beautiful world and to watch over all the plants, trees, birds, fish and animals.

ALL CHILDREN: God made you and me!

To conclude the play children may sing "God's Beautiful World."

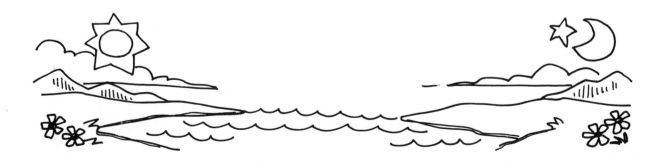

DAVID AND HIS SHEEP

by Marilyn Senterfitt

Cast: Narrator, David, any number of sheep, 2-4 lions

Narrator: David was a young shepherd. He took care of his father's sheep. (*David and sheep enter stage left and walk to center. David carries harp, stick and sling. He sits down and sheep gather around him.*)

David: I really like being a shepherd. God's world is so beautiful!

Sheep: Baa! Baa! (*Loudly.*)

David: On such a beautiful day I like to play my harp. (*Picks up harp and pretends to play. Sheep sway heads back and forth.*)

Sheep: Baa! Baa! (*Softly.*)

David: My sheep like to listen to me play. It quiets them. (*Sheep begin to sit down around David and pretend to sleep.*)

Narrator: It was a beautiful day as David cared for his sheep. Everything was very still. Even the birds did not sing. Suddenly David heard something. (*David puts down harp and picks up stick and sling. Some sheep also stand.*)

David: I thought I heard something move in the trees. (*Points stage right and moves that direction.*)

Sheep: Baa! Baa! (*Very loud.*)

Lions: Roar! Roar! (*Loudly offstage.*)

David: Lions are after my sheep!

(*Lions rush on stage from right. Sheep scatter everywhere. David hurries after them with his stick held high. Chase may take several seconds. Sheep are bleating and lions are roaring. David throws down stick and gets sling. [May be attached to a belt.] At this moment the lions begin to run stage right. David pretends to pick up a stone and circles the sling over his head and "throws" the stone toward stage right. Lions exit.*)

Lions: Roar! Roar! OUCH! (*Loudly offstage.*)

David: Those lions won't bother us again. (*Looks to sky.*) Thank you, Lord, for keeping us safe.

Sheep: Baa! Baa!

(*Sheep gather around David. He sits down and picks up harp and begins to "play" again. Sheep, one by one, sit and go back to sleep. Recorded autoharp music can be softly played offstage.*)

A GOOD MAN

by Marion Schoeberlein

Props: Road scene with trees and grass and a donkey.

Setting the scene: A man (small child) lying near the donkey.

Cast: Priest, Levite, Samaritan (a good man)

Narrator: Jesus told stories to teach us something. He told this story about showing love to our neighbor.

(*Man is lying near donkey groaning. He makes little noises.*)

Priest: (*Passing by.*) This man is sick, but I can't help him. I don't even know him. Let someone else do it. Besides, I don't have time.

(*A little time elapses and then the Levite comes by and notices him.*)

Levite: (*Bending down and looking at him.*) I wonder what happened to this fellow. He must have been robbed. I could help him, but I better not. Maybe the crooks who robbed him are still around.

(*Levite walks down the road, but keeps looking back. Man moans again. Good Samaritan enters slowly and sees the man.*)

Good Samaritan: This poor man was robbed. (*He looks inside a bag next to him.*) There is no money in his money bag. I must help him. (*He pats the man on his head.*)

Good Samaritan: Don't worry. I will help you. (*He gives the man a drink of water from a jug.*)

Good Samaritan: I'll take you to an inn. I'll pay for everything. Here, lean on me.

(*Man gets up and leans on Good Samaritan. They walk slowly away together—the man leaning on the Good Samaritan.*)

Narrator: The good man was the one who helped the man who had been robbed. He was the one who was a neighbor. Jesus wants us all to do the same thing.

GO, JESUS. OBEY YOUR FATHER.

by Catherine Deverell

Between the narrators and chorus an entire class can participate in this.
Time: Long, long ago when Jesus was twelve years old.
Setting: Nazareth and Jerusalem.
This could be done with the children seated in a circle on the floor and all of them taking part in it.

Narrator: God looked down from Heaven. He watched Jesus grow. He helped Jesus learn.

Narrator: Jesus was a good boy. He became strong. He became wise.

God: (*Voice off stage*.) Look at my son. He is a fine boy. Soon He must begin my work on earth.

Chorus: Go, Jesus. Obey your Father.

Narrator: Jesus was twelve years old. His mother and father on earth got ready for a trip.

Mary: I will prepare food to eat on the way.

Joseph: I will pack a few things for our journey. I will load them on the donkey.

Narrator: Mary and Joseph were going to Jerusalem. They were going to the Passover feast.

God: (*Voice off stage*.) My Son must go to Jerusalem with them.

Chorus: Go, Jesus. Obey your Father.

Narrator: In Jerusalem there was a grand temple. It was built in honor of God.

Narrator: People came to the temple to worship God. Teachers came to the temple to teach. They taught the word of God to the people.

God: (*Voice off stage*.) The teachers make me happy. They are very wise. They will help my Son to learn. Jesus must go to the temple.

Chorus: Go, Jesus. Obey your Father.

Jesus: I like Jerusalem. It is a big city. I want to see all of it.

Narrator: Jesus was curious. He wandered through the streets. He looked in the shops.

Narrator: Jesus saw many people—men, women and children who had come to Jerusalem to the Passover feast.

God:	(*Voice off stage.*) These are my people. My Son will be their Savior.
Chorus:	Go, Jesus. Obey your Father.
Narrator:	Jesus came to the temple. He sat down on the steps. He listened to the teachers.
God:	(*Voice off stage.*) Jesus must stay here for a few days. He is my Son. Today He begins His work for me.
Chorus:	Stay, Jesus. Obey your Father.
Narrator:	The Passover feast ended. Mary and Joseph began the journey home. They could not find Jesus.
Mary:	Where is Jesus?
Joseph:	Where is Jesus?
Narrator:	Jesus was not there.
Chorus:	Go, Mary. Find Jesus. Go, Joseph. Find Jesus.
Joseph:	We must go back to Jerusalem.
Mary:	Jesus must have stayed behind. We have to find Him.
Narrator:	For three days Mary and Joseph looked for Jesus. They looked here and there and everywhere. They could not find Him.
Chorus:	Go, Mary. Go to the temple. Go, Joseph. Go to the temple.
Narrator:	Mary and Joseph went to the temple. They found Jesus.
Joseph:	Jesus, why did you stay behind?
Mary:	Joseph and I have been looking for you. We were worried.
Jesus:	I am sorry. I thought you knew. It was my Father's wish. I must begin His work on earth.
Chorus:	Go, Jesus. Obey your Father.
Narrator:	God looked down from heaven.
God:	(*Voice off stage.*) My Son is still a boy. Mary and Joesph will take care of Him. He must go back to Nazareth with them.
Chorus:	Go, Jesus. Obey your Father.
Narrator:	Jesus returned to Nazareth with Mary and Joseph. He grew up and increased in wisdom and faith. The people loved Him. God, His Father, loved Him.
God:	(*Voice off stage.*) This is my Beloved Son. He was born to do my work on earth.
Chorus:	Go, Jesus. Obey your Father.
Narrator:	Jesus always obeyed His Father. He taught the people. He taught children. He loved the people. He loved children.
Chorus:	Go, children. Obey Jesus. 'Cause Jesus loves you.

THE SAD SISTERS

by Katherine D.M. Marko

Cast of Characters: Jesus
    Mary (sister of Lazarus)
    Martha (sister of Lazarus)
    Lazarus
    Isaac and Leah (neighbors) and gardener

Setting: A room with a table, a chair, a bench, shelf or cupboard and hearth. Dress is simple robes for everyone.

Scene I

Narrator: (*At side of stage. Can be an older boy or girl.*) In Bethany a man named Lazarus was sick for several days. Then he died and his sisters, Mary and Martha, were very sad. Jesus had often visited their house but now He was away on a journey.

Mary: (*Looking out window.*) I wish Jesus was here, Martha.

Martha: He will be, Mary. We did send for Him.

Mary: Do you think He could make Lazarus better?

Martha: (*Shaking her head.*) No, it's too late.

(*Mary and Martha cover their faces with their hands. Isaac pats Mary's shoulder. Leah puts her arms around Martha. A knock sounds on the door. Martha answers it and turns to Mary.*)

Martha: Jesus may be coming. I'll see. Wait here. (*She leaves.*)

Isaac: (*To Mary.*) We are very sorry about Lazarus.

Leah:	Yes, it is sad about your brother.
Mary:	Thank you. Won't you sit down?

Curtain

Scene II

Setting: Same as Scene I, about thirty minutes later.

Mary:	(*Going to the widow.*) I hope Jesus comes soon.
Leah:	He will. You can depend on Jesus.

(*Door opens. Martha looks in and beckons to Mary.*)

Mary:	(*Turning to Isaac and Leah.*) I must go. You may wait here if you wish. (*She leaves.*)
Isaac:	(*Rising from bench.*) I wonder where she is going.
Leah:	Maybe to her brother's grave. We should go with her. (*Isaac nods and they both leave.*)

Curtain

Scene III

Setting: Outdoors, in front of tomb. A large cardboard "stone" stands at right rear. Gardener stands near. Jesus, Mary, Martha, Isaac and Leah all enter from left.

Jesus:	(*Pointing at stone.*) Is that where Lazarus is buried?
Martha:	Yes.
Jesus:	Take the stone away. (*Isaac and gardener move stone.*)
Martha:	But he's been in there for four days.
Jesus:	No matter. (*He calls loudly.*) Lazarus, come out.
Lazarus:	(*Coming from behind stone, he rubs his eyes and looks around.*) Jesus, you have saved me. Thank you. (*He looks at his sisters and holds out his arms. They run to him.*)
Mary:	(*Hugs Lazarus; turns to Jesus.*) Oh, thank you, Jesus.
Martha:	(*Also turning to Jesus.*) Yes, thank you Jesus, for bringing him back to us.
Jesus:	(*Smiling at all of them.*) It is good.
Narrator:	(*At side of stage.*) Lazarus was indeed brought back to life. He went on living with his sisters in Bethany. When people heard of the miracle Jesus had performed, many more came to believe in Him. But His enemies were plotting against Him, so he went off to Ephraim and stayed with His disciples.

Curtain

THE GIANT

by Marion Schoeberlein

Cast: David, Goliath, Narrator

Setting: A big field. Goliath, played by a child big for his age, dressed as close to the biblical version of the giant as possible. David may sling a tiny ball out of a slingshot to kill the giant.

Narrator: In Bible times there were many wicked people. They made trouble for the children of Israel. One was a giant by the name of Goliath. Every day he stood out in the fields and bragged about how strong he was. No one wanted to fight him. No one, until a boy by the name of David did.

This is the story of how David killed Goliath.

Goliath: (*Beating on his chest and swaggering around.*) I'm the strongest man in the world. No one can fight me. I can kill ten soldiers at one time.

(*David enters with his slingshot.*)

David: Don't brag, giant. I have come to stop you.

Goliath: (*Swaggering and laughing.*) You are just a little boy. I will pick you up and make a pudding out of you.

David: I will have victory because I have God on my side.

Goliath: Who is that God you talk about? He can't be as strong as I am.

David: My God is Jehovah, the God of EVERYONE.

Goliath: Let's test Him out. If you come near I will squash you like a mouse.

(*David slings the little ball.*)

(*The giant falls to the ground. David comes over and places a foot on his arm.*)

David: I knew I could do it because God was on my side.

Narrator: Lots of people are like the giant in our story. They brag about how strong they are. But if we're smart, we're like David. We trust God to make us strong. Then we're winners.

WHERE YOU GO

by Katherine D.M. Marko

Cast: Naomi
　　　Orpha (Naomi's daughter-in-law)
　　　Ruth (Naomi's daughter-in-law)

Setting: A road leading away from town. Three women are walking along, carrying bundles of belongings. All are dressed in simple robes and head scarfs.

Narrator: (*At side of stage. May be an older boy or girl.*) Naomi had two sons. One married Orpha and the other married Ruth. The sons and their father died, so Naomi, Orpha and Ruth had to leave their home.

Naomi: (*Putting down her bundle on the ground.*) You must go back to your mothers.

Ruth: No, we can't leave you.

Naomi: But I have nothing now.

Orpha: We will stay with you.

Naomi: Why? I have nothing to give you.

Ruth: No matter.

Orpha: We stay.

Naomi: (*She picked up her bundle again. They walk a few steps. She stops again.*) No, this isn't right.

Ruth: But we must take care of you.

Orpha: Yes, we must.

Naomi: (*She puts down her bundle again. So do Orpha and Ruth.*) No, you must go back and marry again.

Orpha: (*She hesitates.*) Well, maybe we should.

Naomi: You should. (*She leans forward and Orpha kisses her cheek.*)

Orpha: Goodbye. Take care. (*She takes her bundle, waves at side of stage and leaves.*)

Naomi: Now, Ruth, you must go, too.

Ruth: (*Shaking her head.*) No, where you go, I go.

Naomi: (*She sighs loudly and nods.*) Then we'll go on together.

Ruth: Yes, where you live I will live.

(*They smile at each other, pick up their bundles and leave.*)

Narrator: (*At side of stage.*) Naomi and Ruth went on to Bethlehem to live. Later Ruth married a relative named Boaz. Ruth and Boaz had a son named Obed, who was the grandfather of King David.

SAUL WAS HIS NAME

by Katherine D.M. Marko

Cast: Saul
      1st Man (friend of Saul)
      2nd Man (friend of Saul)

Setting: A road leading toward Damascus. Three men are walking along quietly. All are dressed in simple robes and sandals.

Scene I

Narrator: (*At side of stage. Can be an older boy or girl.*) Saul had no liking for Christians. He was always plotting against them. He and two friends were now going to Damascus to find Christians whom they could arrest and take back to Jerusalem.

1st Man: Do you think we'll find any Christians?

2nd Man: Yes, I think so.

(*Suddenly a light streaks down around them. A strong flashlight could be used, twirled up and down.*)

Saul: (*Falling to the ground.*) What happened? What happened?

1st Man: Lightning struck you.

2nd Man: Yes, that's what happened.

The Voice: (*Off stage a voice is heard.*) Saul, Saul, why are you against me?

Saul: (*Looking upward from side to side.*) Who are you, Lord? I can't see.

The Voice: I am Jesus.

Saul:	(*Repeating.*) I can't see. I can't see.
The Voice:	Get up and go to the city.
1st Man:	(*Pulling Saul to his feet.*) Come, I'll help you.
Saul:	But my eyes.
2nd Man:	We'll take you to the city.
Saul:	(*Holding tightly to both men.*) So be it. (*They leave.*)

Curtain

Scene II

Setting: Room with table and chairs. Saul sits alone, bent over table holding his head with both hands.

Narrator:	Saul was blind for three days. In Damascus, there was a disciple of Jesus. Jesus told this disciple to go to Saul.

(*A knock on the door is heard.*)

Saul:	(*Lifting his head.*) Who is it?
Disciple:	A friend. Jesus sent me.
Saul:	Come in. (*Door opens. Disciple comes in and places his hands on Saul's head.*)
Disciple:	Jesus sent me so that you will see again.
Saul:	Oh, if I only could.
Disciple:	And He wants you to follow Him.
Saul:	I will. I will. (*He looks around excitedly.*) Oh, I can see. I can see.
Disciple:	Fine, but you must keep your promise.
Saul:	I will. I will follow Jesus forever.
Disciple:	Now I must go. (*He leaves.*)
Saul:	(*He kneels down and prays.*) Oh, Lord, I am sorry I was so wicked.
Narrator:	(*Standing at side of stage.*) Saul stayed a few days in the city of Damascus. Then he was baptized and went about preaching to the people in the name of the Lord. Later he became known as Paul.

Curtain

THE ROCK THAT FOLLOWED THEM

by Laura Cordova

"... for they drank of that spiritual Rock that followed them: and that Rock was Christ."
(I Corinthians 10:4)

Cast: Narrator, child to play the Rock, Moses and three or more Israelites in costume.

Props: Box large enough for a child to fit inside, decorated like a rock, with a door at one end, a rod or stick and cookies (optional).

Setting the scene: Line up Israelites, facing audience, with box in the background, not moving, with door facing the side, away from the audience.

Narrator:	The Israelites had been slaves in Egypt for 250 years. They made bricks from mud and straw that they stomped with their feet.
Israelites:	(*Stomp feet.*) Yucky! Sticky! Squishy!
Narrator:	They wanted a deliverer.
Israelites:	Send us a deliverer!
Narrator:	So God sent Moses.
Moses:	(*Walks in carrying a stick.*) Follow me.
Narrator:	After much persuasion, Moses convinced the king of Egypt to let the Israelites go.

Israelites:	(*Turn to follow Moses and walk around the box. Return to original position and face audience.*)
Narrator:	Suddenly they came to the Red Sea.
Israelites and Moses:	(*Stare at audience with look of surprise.*)
Narrator:	With the sea in front of them and the Egyptian army behind them, they had nowhere to go.
Israelites:	(*Look back, then forward with fear.*)
Narrator:	So Moses raised his rod and the water parted down the middle and they walked through on dry ground.
Israelites:	(*Skip around merrily, praising God.*)
Narrator:	Then the Israelites became hungry and began to whine and complain.
Israelites:	(*Hold out hands to beg.*) Give us bread, give us bread.
Narrator:	And in the morning they found wafers on the ground, called manna.
Israelites:	(*Gather manna. May pretend or use real cookies.*)
Narrator:	But then they were thirsty and they whined and complained again.
Israelites:	Give us water, give us water.
Narrator:	So God said, "Speak to the Rock and it will give you water." But Moses was fed up with the Israelites' complaining and he struck the Rock instead.
Moses:	(*Taps the Rock with his rod.*)
Narrator:	And the Rock gave them water.
Rock:	(*Hands them paper cups through the door and they all pretend to drink.*)
Narrator:	But God was angry with the people and made them walk around and around in the wilderness for forty years.
Israelites:	(*Follow Moses in a large circle.*)
Narrator:	And the Rock followed them.
Rock:	(*Follow Israelites.*)
Narrator:	And they never did make it to the Promised Land. They all died in the wilderness. That is, all except Joshua and Caleb, who led the Israelites' children to their new home.

A SON COMES HOME

by Marilyn Senterfitt

Based on the parable of the Prodigal Son in Luke 15:11-32.

Cast: Narrator, Father, Son, Boy, Girl, several pigs.

Materials: Table, chair, paper plates, craft sticks, two small bags, bucket.

Props: Draw pig face on paper plates and attach ears and craft stick. Fill one bag with pennies.

Setting the scene: Place table and chair stage left. Have filled bag ready stage left. Empty bag and bucket are stage right.

Narrator: Jesus once told a story of a kind father and his restless son. (*Father enters stage left and sits at table. Son enters stage right and walks up to Father.*)

Son: Father, I want to leave home.

Father: What did you say?

Son: I want to go to the big city and have adventures. Please give me my money.

Father: (*Standing.*) I don't want you to go!

Son: I am going, Father. Give me my money.

(*Father, with head down, exits stage left and returns with filled bag. Son looks inside and takes out some coins. Smiling he returns them to bag.*)

Father: Go, if you must!

(*Without a word, Son turns and exits stage right. Father, looking very sad, sits at table. He remains there for rest of play.*)

Narrator: In the big city the Son has a wonderful time, but he soon learns that everything is very expensive.

(*Son enters holding empty bag upside down.*)

Son: Where did it all go? I can't ask my Father for more money. (*Paces back and forth.*) I guess I'll have to find a job.

(*Exits stage right.*)

Narrator: This young man had never worked a day in his life. His father had always done everything for him. What kind of job could he do?

(*Son enters stage right followed by the pigs.*)

Pigs: Oink! Oink!

Son: This is a terrible job!

(*Pretends to feed the pigs from bucket. Pigs oink softly and pretend to eat. They stay close to Son.*)

Son: I wish I could go home, but my father would only laugh at me and send me away.

(*Son sits down among the pigs as they oink and eat.*)

Narrator: What a sad sight. He left a loving father, wasted his money, and now sits among pigs. What a sad sight.

(*Boy and Girl enter stage right and walk by Son and pigs.*)

Boy: (*Points at Son.*) Look at that, Martha. He is sure is a mess!

Girl: (*Holding nose.*) And he smells awful!

(*Walk on exiting stage left.*)

Son: (*Jumping up.*) That does it! I am going home!

(*Exits stage right followed by the pigs oinking loudly. Returns and walks slowly toward Father. Father stands and points toward Son.*)

Father: A stranger is coming up the road. He looks sad in his dirty rags. I'll offer him some food.

(*Starts to exit and then looks at Son again.*)

Father: That's my son!

(*Runs to Son and throws arms around him.*)

Father: My son, my son! You've come home!

Son: Father, I am ashamed. Let me work for you like one of your servants.

Father: You are home. That is all that matters. We are going to have a party! This is a time of great happiness!

(*Father and Son exit, arm in arm, stage left.*)

THE TREES CHOOSE A KING

by Marilyn Senterfitt

Objective: To teach children that God has a purpose for all His creation. Based on Jotham's parable found in Judges 9:7-15.

Materials: You will need tree branches, construction paper and posters.

Cast: A king, several soldiers, children holding tree branches, an olive tree, fig tree, grapevine, thornbush, raven and a narrator. Only the narrator will speak.

Props: Tree branches should be from a variety of trees. Collect on the day of the play or keep in water. Use construction paper to make an olive tree, fig tree, grapevine and thornbush to glue on posters as shown. King may wear a crown and soldiers can carry swords all made from poster board.

Setting the scene: King and soldiers wait offstage to left. Trees with branches stand apart at center stage. Thornbush sits near the front of the stage. The olive tree and grapevine stand apart stage right and the fig tree stands stage left. As the play begins, the raven "flies" on stage and kneels beside the child representing a cedar tree. Children hold up their posters or tree branches throughout the narration.

Narrator: It was a beautiful day as the wind blew the trees of the forest. (*Tree branches gently sway.*) The king and his soldiers from the great city enjoyed riding through the forest. (*King and soldiers "ride" among the trees and then exit stage right.*) The trees were in awe of the king and his riches and power. That very day they decided that the trees should have a king also.

The juniper called to the raven who was busily building a nest in the cedar tree. "Mrs. Raven, we want you to go to the olive grove on the small hill outside the city. Find the best olive tree and ask it to be our king." (*Raven nods head up and down and "flies" to the olive tree standing stage right.*)

The raven asked the olive tree if he would agree to be king of all the trees but the olive tree said "no." (*Olive tree moves poster side to side indicating "no."*) He did not want to stop making olives for the humans and just wave to and fro over the other trees. (*Raven "flies" back to the trees.*)

The trees were very sad when they heard the raven's report. The oak had another suggestion. He said, "Mrs. Raven, fly swiftly to the fig tree in nearby Bethany. It is greatly admired and will make an excellent king." The raven once again flew away. (*Raven "flies" to the fig tree standing stage left.*)

The raven asked her question and the fig tree also said "no!" (*Nods poster side to side.*) She wanted to do nothing more than grow sweet fruit for the humans. She liked being just where she was. The raven quickly returned to the trees. ("*Flies*" *back.*)

Now the trees were very disappointed, but the oak had yet another suggestion. He said, "We must look elsewhere for our king. The humans like the grapevine. He would be a worthy king of the trees."

For the third time the raven was sent out. (*Flies to the grapevine standing stage right.*) She said, "I am here to ask if you will be king of all the trees. Will you accept this great honor?" The grapevine did not hesitate and replied, "No, I think not. I enjoy producing fruit for the humans, I want no other life." (*Raven "flies" back.*)

The raven's wings were growing weary. Surely they would not send her out another time. The trees were about to give up in their search for a king when the pine tree spoke up. He said, "We could ask the thornbush to be our king."

All the trees cried at once, "The thornbush!" (*Branches rustle wildly.*) The oak continued, "That terrible thing is not worthy to be a king. Even the humans don't like it." Since no one could think of anyone else to ask, the trees agreed to send the raven once more. (*Raven "flies" to stage front and the thornbush.*)

The raven was very careful around the thornbush. She did not want to be caught in his sharp thorns. She asked if he would be king of the trees and the thornbush laughed and replied, "How desperate the trees must be to ask the lowly thornbush. Of course, I will accept this honor, but first the trees must do something for me." The raven did not like the sound of this and asked what it was. The thornbush answered, "All the trees must bow low to me so that I alone provide shade in the forest."

The weary raven flew back to the trees and gave the thornbush's reply. The trees were delighted. (*Branches sway to and fro.*) "Now we will have a king just like the humans!" cried the oak.

Suddenly, the cedar, who was the oldest and wisest of all the trees, spoke, "You fools! Don't you see if you bow down to the thornbush he will cover you with his thorny branches. In time the humans will come to the forest and destroy the thornbush and all of you along with it!"

The other trees held their heads down. (*Bow branches.*) They had so wanted to be like the humans they had been willing to bow down to a dangerous enemy. The oak thanked the raven for her efforts and she returned to her nest building. (*"Flies" to place beside the cedar and kneels.*) All the trees looked up at the beautiful sky above. The wind blew gently through their uplifted branches. (*Hold branches up and sway gently.*) Never again did the trees search for a king. They were now content to live in the world of the humans, providing them with food for their tables, wood for their fires, cooling shade in the heat of summer, and great beauty all year round. (*King and soldiers enter stage right and ride to the trees and "dismount," sitting among the trees. Trees continue to sway branches back and forth.*)

(All children may say this short poem to close play or sing an appropriate song such as "God's Beautiful World.")

>Let all the creation cry,
>"Glory to the Lord on high!"

>Let all the creation sing,
>"God alone can be our king!"

MOSES CHOSEN

by Virginia L. Kroll

Cast of Characters: Narrator
Moses
Voice of God

Setting: Outdoors

Time: Daylight

At Rise: Narrator walks on stage and points to burning bush.

Narrator: Look, oh look, the bush is burning, all the leaves are ablaze. Moses comes to see it closely through the heated haze.

(*Moses enters, stops and studies the bush, then edges closer slowly.*)

Moses: How can this happen? What a strange sight! The leaves are still green though the fire burns bright.

Voice: (*Off stage.*) Take off your sandals; this is holy ground. (*Moses removes his shoes, then covers his face.*)

Moses: Oh, I'm so frightened I can't turn around.

Voice: (*Off stage.*) Moses, I came on this mountain to you; there is a great task I'd like you to do.

Moses: Goodness, oh, how can it be that my God has chosen me?

Voice: (*Off stage.*) Look up from the stones and sand; listen now to my command. (*Moses looks up to the direction of the Voice.*) You will go to Egypt and free my people from that land. Lead them from their cares and woes to where the milk and honey flows.

Moses: God, forgive me, but how can you expect this from one man? Such a burden, such a chore! (*Moses throws up his hands in despair.*) Who'll believe my words, what's more?

Voice: (*Off stage.*) I'll be with you as you go. Many victories will you know. (*Moses stands still. Narrator enters and stands center stage.*)

Narrator: Moses listened and obeyed. Moses spoke to God and prayed, winning all the freedom fights, leader of the Israelites.

(*Narrator exits.*)

THE MAN IN THE TREE

by Marion Schoeberlein

Props: Tree made out of very stiff cardboard—with branches for a child to sit in, or behind on a ladder, as though perched in tree.

Setting the scene: Child playing Zacchaeus is sitting in branches of the tree. Child playing Jesus and children (about eight or ten) playing followers of Jesus and disciples enter stage slowly.

Characters: Jesus, Zacchaeus, some disciples and followers of Jesus

Costumes: Robes and headpieces

Narrator: (*Child of six or seven.*) Jesus is everybody's friend. In Bible times He made a special friend. His name was Zacchaeus. Zacchaeus was a very little man. He sometimes stole people's money, so no one liked him. One day he heard Jesus was coming to his city. He wanted to see Jesus. But he was so short he couldn't because the other people were so tall. Zacchaeus climbed into a tree. Jesus saw him in the tree and told him to come down. Then they were friends.

Zacchaeus: I can see Jesus now. I'm afraid. They say He is everybody's friend, but He won't like me.

Jesus: (*Walking slowly over to the tree.*) Little man, come down from the tree. I want to talk to you.

Zacchaeus: What do you want with me?

Jesus: I know all about you. I know how you stole tax money. But I want to come to your house and eat supper with you.

Zacchaeus: But why, Lord?

Jesus: Because I want to save you.

(*People begin to grumble.*)

Person in
the crowd: He is a sinner, Jesus!

(*Zacchaeus climbs down from the tree and stands at Jesus' feet.*)

Zacchaeus: I'm sorry for what I did, Jesus. I will not steal anymore. I will pay back all the money.

Jesus: Yes, Zacchaeus, you will.

Zacchaeus: Are you really my friend now?

Jesus: Yes, I am. I will always be your friend.

(*The crowd exits from one side of the stage. Jesus and Zacchaeus exit from the other.*)

NOAH AND HIS NEIGHBORS

by Virginia L. Kroll

Cast: Noah, 11 neighbors, 3 sons, 4 wives

Costumes: Noah wears a simple robe, as do his sons. His wife and his sons' wives wear long skirts or dresses in plain colors. Noah has a beard. The neighbors should be in colorful clothes, perhaps outrageously garbed, to show worldliness.

Properties: A hammer for Noah and sacks of food or boxes of food for all the wives and sons; an ark that is large enough to hide 8 persons standing behind it, perhaps a painted cardboard cutout.

Setting: Outside, biblical times

Time: Daylight

At Rise: Noah is making hammering motions on his ark as if building.

(*Neighbor 1 enters.*)

Neighbor 1: Hammer, hammer, hammer, pound, pound, pound. Noah, why're you making all that building sound?

Noah: Hammer, hammer, hammer, nail, nail, nail. I have been commanded by our Lord to sail.

(*Neighbor 2 enters.*)

Neighbor 2: Sail, sail, sail? Whither will you go? There is not a drop of water here, you know.

Noah: Water, water, water. Never question God. Here will flow a river (*Noah waves his hand to indicate a wide area of ground*) washing o'er the sod.

(*Neighbor 3 enters.*)

Neighbor 3: I do not believe you; you are telling tales. Next you'll be imagining fish and shrimp and whales!

(*Neighbors 4, 5 and 6 enter.*)

Noah: Tales, tales, tales? My lips do not lie! God has said He'll wash away all this land now dry.

Neighbor 4:	Who told you of this promise? How do you claim to know? You make me laugh with silly words. Oh, how you blabber so!
Noah:	Into my ears, God's voice one day became a roaring sound, telling of the wickedness in all men He'd found.
Neighbor 5:	Everyone, he's crazy! Is it any wonder? He pretends he heard the Lord in a clap of thunder.
Neighbor 6:	Crazy, crazy, crazy, all of us agree. (*Points upward.*) Look, the sun is out now, bright and shining, see?
Noah:	Hammer, hammer, hammer. I've work to complete. Animals I've gathered need much food to eat. (*Noah looks to one side of stage and beckons with his hand.*) Sons and wives, come hither (*Noah's wife, 3 sons, and 3 wives enter, carrying sacks of food*). Soon you must come aft, saved from rain's destruction upon this mighty raft. (*Noah pats the ark.*) Finished, finished, finished. (*Noah cups his ear and listens.*) Quiet, and all hark! Sh, I hear the rumbling. Quick, aboard the ark! (*Noah, wives, and sons hide behind ark as if entering it. Neighbors 7, 8, 9, 10 and 11 enter, joining other neighbors.*)
Neighbor 7:	Silly, silly, silly, climbing on a ship that is going nowhere. What a wasted trip!
Neighbor 8:	Listen, listen, listen! (*Cupping hand over ear and cocking head.*) What's that tapping sound?
Neighbor 9:	Rain is heading toward us. (*Looks up and turns palms upwards to feel rain.*) Hear it, feel it pound!
Neighbor 10:	Flooding, flooding, flooding, every barn and stall. (*Ark moves off stage.*)
Neighbor 11:	Noah wasn't kidding, was he, after all? (*All kneel and bow heads in prayer.*)

LOST AND FOUND

by Clara Burton Smith

Cast: Narrator, Rachel, Aaron, woman selling jars, seller (boy) of sweets, girl in crowd, Voice, Jesus, crowd.

Scene I

The Marketplace: Two tables to represent booths, one with objects that can pass for trays of sweets, the other with a few jars or pottery.

When scene opens, several children may be seen standing near or strolling past booths. Jar seller stands behind her booth; sweets seller stands behind his booth.

As the narrator begins, Rachel and Aaron enter from stage right.

Narrator: Rachel and Aaron went to the market place. Rachel held tightly to her brother's hand, but Aaron struggled to pull his hand away. Mother said that they could go to the market if Rachel was sure to hold Aaron's hand.

Rachel: Aaron, Mama said that you must hold my hand.

Narrator: But Aaron complained. He said he could walk by himself because he was four years old.

Aaron: I'm big! I'm four years old!

Narrator: Rachel loved her brother very much, but he could be a problem. She told him that he wasn't big enough yet.

Rachel: You're big, but not quite big enough.

Narrator: The market was exciting. There were lots of good things to eat. Everything looked and smelled delicious. The children went from one booth to the other. Aaron smelled something good.

Aaron: (*Sniffing.*) Mmmmmmmm . . . something smells good!

Rachel: (*Sniffing.*) Mmmmmmmm . . . my favorite date cakes!

(*Both children stand and look over the goodies.*)

Narrator: Mother had given Rachel some coins to buy a treat for each of them. But it was so hard to choose. They looked and looked, then moved to the next booth. There were all kinds of water jars. They were so nice. Mother's jar was old. It would be such fun to buy her a new one for a surprise.

Rachel: We could buy Mama a new water jar!

(*Children stand looking and pointing to the jars.*)

Narrator: The two saw the woman at the booth. Rachel took the coins from her pocket while Aaron watched but she still held his hand. Then Rachel showed the woman the coins.

Rachel:	Is this enough to buy a water jar?
Narrator:	The woman shook her head. Rachel and Aaron were so disappointed. Then Rachel had an idea. They could save up their coins.
Rachel:	(*To Aaron.*) We can save up our money until we come again.
Narrator:	Aaron smiled. He was happy that they would be able to surprise Mama.
Aaron:	Next time we'll get a jar for Mama.

(*Rachel and Aaron continue across stage.*)

Narrator:	As they neared the end of the market, Rachel tripped. For the first time, she let go of her brother's hand. She told him to wait.
Rachel:	Wait till I fix my sandal, Aaron.
Narrator:	Rachel bent down to tie her sandal. Just as she stood up, Aaron ran off toward the city gate. He was laughing and calling to Rachel to catch him.
Aaron:	Catch me, Rachel, catch me! (*Aaron runs off stage left.*)
Narrator:	Rachel took off after him, calling him to come back.
Rachel:	Come back, come back, you'll get lost! (*Rachel runs off stage as she calls Aaron.*)

Curtain

Scene II

Stage is clear except for bench at center of stage where Jesus is seated.

When scene opens, children are standing in groups toward front of stage. Some children may carry dolls wrapped in blankets to represent mothers and their babies.

Narrator:	Rachel was terrified. She looked everywhere for her brother until finally she saw a small figure running toward a crowd gathered on the side of a hill.

(*Rachel enters left, looking all around.*)

Narrator:	Rachel looked around the edge of the crowd. Aaron must be somewhere among all those people. She asked a girl standing near her why there was such a big crowd of people.
Rachel:	What is happening?
Narrator:	The girl told Rachel that the great teacher, Jesus, was there.

Girl: It's Jesus. He is preaching here.

(*Everyone moves to the rear center stage to see Jesus.*)

Narrator: Rachel followed the other children. Could it be the great teacher her father talked about? As she came closer she heard some of Jesus' followers scolding the children for interrupting the lesson.

Voice: The Master is busy preaching. You must not disturb Him!

Narrator: Rachel stood still; she was afraid. Then a strong, clear voice rang out.

Jesus: Let the children come to me and do not stop them. Come, children, come.

Narrator: Jesus spread His arms and the children gathered around Him.

(*Children sit down in a circle around Jesus. Rachel stands and stares.*)

Narrator: Rachel just stood still. She was staring at a little boy sitting at Jesus' feet. It was her own brother. He saw Rachel and ran to her and took her hand leading her to Jesus.

Aaron: Rachel, Rachel, come and see!

(*Aaron leads Rachel to Jesus and they sit before Him.*)

Narrator: Rachel saw Jesus' bright eyes and kind smile. His voice was gentle as He spoke to the children.

Jesus: (*Lifting His arms.*) Let the little children come unto me and forbid them not, for such is the kingdom of heaven.

(*Jesus goes from child to child laying His hand on the head of each one. Mothers hold up their babies for a blessing.*)

Narrator: Lovingly, Jesus blessed every child. Rachel was no longer afraid. When it was time to go, Aaron reached for Rachel's hand.

(*Other children rise and leave stage right, waving at Jesus as they go. Jesus stands at rear center of stage waving at the children. Rachel and Aaron go to front of stage, look back and wave.*)

Rachel: (*Hugging Aaron.*) You're a good boy, Aaron.

Narrator: But Aaron looked worried. He wondered if Mama and Papa would be angry with him for running away from Rachel.

Aaron: Will Mama and Papa be mad at me?

Rachel: No, Aaron, Mama and Papa will be happy when I tell them how we found Jesus.

Narrator: They forgot all about the treats and the water jar. All they could think about was their wonderful new friend who loved children so much. Hand in hand they skipped all the way home.

(*Rachel and Aaron skip off stage right.*)

Curtain

THE LADY WHO TURNED INTO SALT

by Marion Schoeberlein

Cast: Two angels, Lot, two daughters, Lot's wife, Narrator

Setting: City scene painted on cardboard

Narrator: In Bible times there was a big city with lots of people in it. The name of it was Sodom. God looked down on this city and saw that it was very bad. Hardly anyone believed in God. "I will burn up this city," God said. There was one family, though, in Sodom that was good. This is the story of what happened to this family.

Two Angels: (*First angel talking to Lot.*) God sent us to you.

Lot: Why has He sent you?

Two Angels: (*Second angel talking to Lot.*) God is going to burn up this city.

Lot: Why, when it is so beautiful?

First angel: Because the people are bad. He sent us to tell you to go away from here. He said to hurry—before the fire starts. And be sure not to look back when you leave.

Lot: (*Turning and speaking to his wife and daughters.*) You heard the angels. We have to leave right away. God is angry with this city.

(*Lot's daughters start to cry.*)

Lot's wife: But I can't leave all my things here.

Lot: We must do as God said. (*Lot takes her by the arm. The two daughters follow. Then Lot's wife turns and looks back. She keeps standing there while Lot and his daughters walk on. Lot's wife is dressed in white so she looks more like a pillar of salt.*)

Narrator: Lot's wife did not obey God or her husband. She wanted to stay in Sodom. She kept looking back, so God turned her into a pillar of salt. After that, fire came out of heaven and burned the whole city.

MARY AND MARTHA

by Marion Schoeberlein

Setting the scene: Home scene. Mary is sitting by the table. Martha is setting it.

Characters: Mary, Martha and Jesus

Narrator: Jesus had two friends. Their names were Mary and Martha. They were sisters who loved Jesus very much. Both of them loved Him in their own way. Jesus knew that. But when He came to visit, He told them which one loved Him the way He wanted to be loved.

Martha: Mary, come and help me set the table. I can't do all this work by myself.

Mary: Yes, Martha. I'm glad Jesus is coming today to visit.

Martha: Do you think He will like these figs and grapes?

Mary: Jesus always likes our food.

Martha: I wonder if He will want bread to eat.

Mary: Maybe.

Martha: I think I hear footsteps outside. That must be Him.

(*Jesus comes in.*)

Jesus: It's so good to see you again, Mary and Martha.

Mary: So good, Jesus.

Martha: Sit down, Jesus.

(*Jesus sits down. Mary sits down next to him. Martha keeps setting the table.*)

Jesus: Mary, what are you thinking of?

Mary: How you teach us more and more every time you come.

Jesus: Thank you, Mary. Are you remembering the things I teach?

Mary: Oh yes, I think about them all the time.

Martha: That's all she ever does, Jesus. Think and dream all day long. I wish she would help me with the work more. I've worked all morning long making a nice meal for You. Tell her to help me, Jesus.

Jesus: Martha, I always love coming here. I know how hard you work. But when Mary sits at my feet listening to my Word she is doing the right thing. I don't come for a meal. I come because I want to teach both of you my Word.

(*Martha sits down, too.*)

Martha: Then I'll sit down and listen, too.

(*Mary smiles.*)

Jesus: Good. Now I can teach both of you. I know both of you love me. That's why I come to visit and tell you God's Word.

Narrator: When Jesus came to visit, Martha learned the best thing was to listen to what Jesus had to say.

MARY'S ANGEL

by Marion Schoeberlein

Props: Painted scenery of a garden

Setting the scene: Mary is kneeling in the garden, picking flowers.

Characters: Mary and the Angel

Narrator: Before Jesus was born, an angel came to Mary. He told Mary she would have a son. His name would be called Jesus. He would save everyone.

Mary: I hear something. A noise. What is it?

(*Angel comes slowly into the garden.*)

Angel: Mary, don't be afraid.

Mary: Who are you?

Angel: I am sent from God.

Mary: Why did He send you?

Angel: He sent me to tell you that you are going to be a Mother.

Mary: But I'm not married.

Angel: That's all right. God can make it come true.

Mary: Tell me about the Child.

Angel: Your child will be a Son. His name will be Jesus. He will be great. He will save all His people from sin.

(*Angel leaves and Mary rises.*)

Mary: I am so blessed. The Lord is good to me. The angel said He could make it come true. And I believe the angel. Oh, Lord God, I feel so humble. I am your servant. You can bring it to pass.

Narrator: After the angel left she spoke to God in a long prayer. It was a prayer of joy. Mary must have felt like the happiest woman in the whole world.

THE CAMELS AND THE CHRISTMAS PLAY

by Virginia Hoppes

Cast of Characters:
    Narrator
    play director
    Mary
    Joseph
    a doll to represent Baby Jesus
    a chorus of angels
    three wise men
    three camels
    Janitor

Setting: A Nativity scene at the center of the stage.

(*The play director enters first and shows the other players where to stand. Mary and Joseph take their place at the manger. Singers dressed as angels stand on both sides of the Nativity scene.*)

Narrator: The actors and actresses met to rehearse
                The annual Christmas play held at the church.
                There was Mary and Joseph, the angels close by,
                The babe in the manger, the star in the sky.

(*First wise man enters, carrying a gift and leading his camel, Glori, to the right side of Nativity scene. The play director motions directions.*)

Narrator: The wise men and camels then entered the scene.
                One camel, named Glori, was calm and serene.
                She'd been in the play for three years in a row
                And knew every scene and routine in the show.

(*Other two wise men enter, leading their camels and carrying gifts. They move to left side of Nativity scene. The play director motions directions, then sits in his director's chair at the right side of the stage.*)

Narrator: The other two camels, however, were new.
                They'd never before been away from the zoo.
                The man who had brought those two camels had claimed
                As far as he knew they had never been named.

                Both camels were nervous that very first day
                But they tried to cooperate, tried to obey,
                As Glori would demonstrate what they should do.
                The chorus sang "Gloria"; that was her cue.

(*First wise man and Glori walk to the manger while chorus sings "Gloria in Excelsis." Wise man gives gift to Mary. Wise man and camel kneel.*)

Narrator: She marched to the music—a slow steady pace,
                And under the spotlight she stopped at her place.
                She knelt by the baby who lay on the hay,
                Then sat very still till the end of the play.

(*Chorus sings first verse and refrain of "We Three Kings." Other two wise men and camels move to manger on cue. Wise men present gifts to Mary. Then wise men and camels kneel.*)

Narrator: The other two camels then did the same things.
One learned that his cue was the song, "We Three Kings."
The other one waited to take his turn, too.
The verse, "Star of Wonder," was his special cue.
They knelt at that lovely Nativity scene;
A wondrous moment that seemed like a dream,
With the warmth from the Christmas star shining above
And the feeling of being surrounded with love.

(*Chorus hums "Silent Night."*)

Narrator: The play was performed every night for two weeks,
And after the last play the cast stayed for treats.
They petted the animals, thanking them each,
And then the director delivered a speech.

(*The camels move to the side of the stage and all the cast sit on the floor except for two or three who serve cookies. Speech can be read by the play director or by Narrator as play director pantomimes speaking to the camels.*)

Narrator or Play Director:
You're two fine camels; it's a shame
That none of you have a name.
We've all just called you "One" and "Two,"
But that's not good enough for you.
We've thought about it and we knew
You've always listened for your cue;
So even though the play is done,
We'll call you king now, Camel-One.

And Camel-Two, we've named you Star.
A superstar is what you are.
These names are on this plaque for you
To take home with you to the zoo.

You camels, don't forget your cues,
Because, of course, we'd like to use
The three of you in next year's play.
Now have a happy holiday.

(*Play director hold up plaque. Everyone applauds. Glori bows, then other two camels bow.*)

Narrator: When she heard the applause, Glori made a great bow.
She'd worked for the circus and so she knew how.
And then Star and King bowed the very same way.
Those camels were proud to be part of that play.

And now it was late. Time to go home and rest.
The people agreed this year's play was the best.
They promised the camels they'd visit the zoo
And go the circus to see Glori, too.

(*Players leave stage waving to the camels and calling, "Good-bye, Star," "Good-bye, King," "Good-bye, Glori," "Merry Christmas!" The camels then sit down by the manger. The janitor enters, sweeping the floor.*)

Narrator: When everyone else left the party
The janitor came in and saw
The camels were sitting there guarding
The baby who lay on the straw.

WE TRUST IN GOD

by Ellen Javernick

Backdrop: Rainbow of hand prints on sheet

(Daniel 6)
Narrator:
The other princes were jealous because King Darius loved Daniel so much. They wanted to get rid of Daniel, but he was kind and good and they knew he would never do anything to displease the king. Then the princes thought of an idea. They tricked King Darius into signing a law stating that any person who worshiped someone other than the king would be put into the lions' den. Although Daniel knew about the law, he prayed to God. The king had no choice but to throw Daniel into the lions' den. Daniel was not afraid. He knew that God would take care of him and sure enough God did. In the morning, Daniel was safe; King Darius made a new law that said that everyone in his kingdom should worship Daniel's God.

Cast of characters: Daniel in bathrobe with towel turban
lions with yellow paper plate masks on sticks

Singers: (To the tune of "If You're Happy and You Know It")

Daniel in the lions' den wasn't afraid.
Daniel in the lions' den wasn't afraid.
He knew that God was there,
And he trusted in His care.
Daniel in the lions' den wasn't afraid.

(Jonah 1-2)
Narrator:
When Jonah was traveling in a ship, the ocean got very rough. The sailors thought that the storm was Jonah's fault. They threw Jonah into the sea. A whale swallowed Jonah. Inside the whale Jonah was not afraid. He prayed that God would take care of him and sure enough He did. The whale coughed Jonah up onto the shore.

Actors: Children holding whale cut from cardboard box and painted. Additional children can be walking behind other fish-shaped boxes. Jonah, covered with green crepe paper seaweed, walks behind whale.

Singers: Jonah in the whale wasn't afraid.
Jonah in the whale wasn't afraid.
He knew that God was there,
And he trusted in His care.
Jonah in the whale wasn't afraid.

(Genesis 6-9)
People had not been following God's rules. This made God sad. God told Noah that he was going to send a flood to cover the land. He told Noah to build an ark and to bring two of each kind of animal into the ark. Noah did as God told him to. The big flood came. It lasted a long time but Noah did not worry. He knew that God would take care of him, and sure enough He did. At last the flood stopped and the water dried up.

Actors: Children holding ark cut from heavy cardboard; Noah dressed in robe. Additional children can stand behind the ark holding paper plate animal masks.

Singers: Noah in the ark wasn't afraid.
Noah in the ark wasn't afraid.
He knew that God was there,
And he trusted in His care.
Noah in the ark wasn't afraid.

(Additional scenes could include:
When David saw Goliath, he wasn't afraid.
The Disciples in the storm weren't afraid.)

Finale:
(*All children come out and hold hands and sing.*)

When things go wrong for me, I'm not afraid.
When things go wrong for me, I'm not afraid.
I know that God is there,
And I trust in His care.
When things go wrong for me, I'm not afraid.

CHRISTMAS FINALE

by Helen Kitchell Evans

This may be sung by an adult, older youth group, or large group of children of all ages. It could be used as a reading if the director wished.

As the verses are read, or sung, the very youngest in the educational department could do the pictorial parts.

1. Child carries doll on stage.
2. Child carries a large cardboard star covered with silver.
3. Several shepherds walk on stage.
4. Three wise men come on stage; others could follow carrying luggage needed on a trip.
5. Children carry animal cutouts they have made. Should be about the size of construction paper, attached to a stick for holding over head as they walk in. Rulers would do very well.
6. Two children walk a large cardboard donkey on stage.
7. Scene is formed; Mary holding Jesus (spotlight on them).
8. Joseph comes into the scene with Mary and Jesus.
9. Child carries in myrrh.
10. Child carries a pot of gold.
11. Child brings in frankincense. Too dangerous to have it burning so spray sweet perfume over the frankincense to bring in odor of incense.
12. Many children enter wearing crowns of joy. These could be similar to crowns of angels. Children might have their own ideas about a crown of joy, some may want flowers (silk or plastic, etc.). Get their ideas and try to use them here.

On the first night of Christmas
Our great Lord gave to me,
A dear little baby to see.

On the second night of Christmas
Our great Lord gave to me,
One shiny star,
And a dear little baby to see.

On the third night of Christmas
Our great Lord gave to me,
Shepherds in a field,
One shiny star,
And a dear little baby to see.

On the fourth night of Christmas
Our great Lord gave to me,
Wise men of old,
Shepherds in a field,
One shiny star,
And a dear little baby to see.

On the fifth night of Christmas
Our great Lord gave to me,
Animals standing near,
Wise men of old,
Shepherds in a field,
One shiny star,
And a dear little baby to see.

On the sixth night of Christmas
Our great Lord gave to me,
A donkey waiting there,
Animals standing near,
Wise men of old,
Shepherds in a field,
One shiny star,
And a dear little baby to see.

On the seventh night of Christmas
Our great Lord gave to me,
Mary holding Jesus,
A donkey waiting there,
Animals standing near,
Wise men of old,
Shepherds in a field,
One shiny star,
And a dear little baby to see.

On the eighth night of Christmas
Our great Lord gave to me,
Joseph standing close,
Mary holding Jesus,
A donkey waiting there,
Animals standing near,
Wise men of old,
Shepherds in a field,
One shiny star,
And a dear little baby to see.

On the ninth night of Christmas
Our great Lord gave to me,
Sweet smelling myrrh,
Joseph standing close,
Mary holding Jesus,
A donkey waiting there,
Animals standing near,
Wise men of old,
Shepherds in a field,
One shiny star,
And a dear little baby to see.

On the tenth night of Christmas
Our great Lord gave to me,
Bright shining gold,
Sweet smelling myrrh,
Joseph standing close,
Mary holding Jesus,
A donkey waiting there,
Animals standing near,
Wise men of old,
Shepherds in a field,
One shiny star,
And a dear little baby to see.

On the eleventh night of Christmas
Our great Lord gave to me,
Nice frankincense,
Bright shining gold,
Sweet smelling myrrh,

Joseph standing close,
Mary holding Jesus,
A donkey waiting there,
Animals standing near,
Wise men of old,
Shepherds in a field,
One shiny star,
And a dear little baby to see.

On the twelveth night of Christmas
Our great Lord gave to me,
A crown of joy,
Nice frankincense,
Bright shining gold,
Sweet smelling myrrh,
Joseph standing close,
Mary holding Jesus,
A donkey waiting there,
Animals standing near,
Wise men of old,
Shepherds in a field,
One shiny star,
And a dear little baby to see.

Finish this with a parade of the Twelve Nights of Christmas through the congregation while music is played either live or recorded.